# Looking Forward

## Participatory Economics for the Twenty First Century

**Michael Albert
&
Robin Hahnel**

**Looking Forward: Participatory
Economics for the Twenty First Century**

Graphics by Matt Wuerker
Cover design by Michael Albert
Cover art by Fernand Leger, *The Great Parade*
Designed and produced by Michael Albert

Manufactured in the USA

Library of Congress Cataloging in Publication Data

Albert, Michael, 1947-
 Looking Forward: participatory economics for the twenty first
century / Michael Albert and Robin Hahnel.
       p.    cm.
 Includes bibliographical references.
 ISBN 0-89608-406-X (cloth) : $25.00. — ISBN 0-89608-405-1
(pbk.) : $10.00
 1. Economics. 2. Welfare economics. 3. Comparative economics.
4. Distributive Justice. 5. Industrial management—Employee participation. 6. Economic policy—Citizen participation.
I. Hahnel, Robin. II. Title. III. Title: Participatory economics.
HB171.A415  1991                                          91-
474
330—dc20                                                  CIP

**South End Press, 116 Saint Botolph Street, Boston, MA 02115**
**98 97 96 95 94**                              **2 3 4 5 6 7 8 9**

*There was only one catch and that was Catch-22, which specified that a concern for one's own safety in the face of dangers that were real and immediate was the process of a rational mind. Orr was crazy and could be grounded. All he had to do was ask; and as soon as he did, he would no longer be crazy and would have to fly more missions....If he flew them he was crazy and didn't have to; but if he didn't want to he was sane and had to.... 'That's some catch, that Catch-22,' Yossarian observed. 'It's the best there is,' Doc Daneeka agreed.*

—*Joseph Heller*
Catch-22

*To doubt everything or to believe everything are two equally convenient solutions; both dispense with the necessity of reflection.*

—*Bertrand Russell*
Science and Method

*I wish that every human life might be pure transparent freedom.*

—*Simone de Beauvoir*
The Blood of Others

# Table Of Contents

# Prologue

*The familiar notion of planning is that done by experts, with scientific knowledge. We have seen the results of that rational planning: tower blocks, food additives, valium—the list of horrors is endless.*

*Sheila Rowbotham*

The eleven chapters of this book describe an economic system relevant to many times and places. We do not discuss specific existing economies, but we cannot entirely ignore *glasnost*, *perestroika,* the recent dramatic events in Eastern Europe, and contemporary claims of "the triumph of capitalism."

If what is crumbling in the East is the only possible alternative to capitalism, as many people believe, then trying to develop a different economic vision is futile. On the other hand, if what is crumbling is only one horribly flawed alternative to capitalism, as a minority of critics have been claiming since 1917, trying to find a superior alternative makes sense. This prologue is for readers who are not convinced that seeking alternatives is a worthwhile pursuit. Others may want to proceed directly to the introduction which begins on page 11.

"*In capitalism, capitalists own the means of production, use markets for allocation, define the purpose and character of work, and hire and fire workers (and managers)."*

## Capitalism Triumphant?

Robert Heilbroner, a respected leftist professor at the New School of Social Research, and author of numerous widely-read books on economics, has decided to lend his considerable literary skills to advancing the pessimistic interpretation of recent events. In *New Perspectives Quarterly* (Fall 1989), Heilbroner asserts that, "Less than 75 years after the contest between capitalism and socialism officially began, it is over: capitalism has won." According to Heilbroner, "the tumultuous changes taking place in the Soviet Union, China, and Eastern Europe have given us the clearest possible proof that capitalism organizes the material affairs of humankind more satisfactorily than socialism." And though Heilbroner doesn't proclaim, as others do, that this means we have reached the "end of history" he does say that "we are finally coming

*"We believe a new economy can be built that embodies humane values and functions efficiently. How do we retain such optimistic conclusions despite Heilbroner's celebration of capitalism's 'triumph'? Certainly not by denying the facts all around us."*

to grips with the end of the economic century. From now on, the main problems will not be economic, but cultural and political."

In short, for Heilbroner only two types of economic system are possible: what we have in the West (which Heilbroner calls capitalism) and what they had in the East (which Heilbroner calls socialism). Since the East is dead, Heilbroner concludes that while egalitarian goals are nice, they are unachievable, and that while capitalism isn't perfect, it's what works.

Yet from Chicago's capitalist ghettos, to New York's capitalist unemployment lines, to Los Angeles's capitalist emergency wards, to Houston's capitalist dirty alleys—from capitalist Seattle to capitalist Sarasota and from capitalist Dallas to capitalist Detroit—it is increasingly clear that "everything is broken," not only politically and culturally, but also *economically.*

Growing inequality. Rampant homelessness. Voracious militarism. Crime. Cultural commodification. Ecological dissolution. Alienation. Addiction. These are the coin of modern capitalism, evident in every city in the United States.

We believe a new economy can be built that embodies humane values *and* functions efficiently. How do we retain such optimistic conclusions despite Heilbroner's celebration of capitalism's "triumph"? Certainly not by denying the facts all around us.

The Soviet economy can't enrich Moscow's elites much less its downtrodden, but does this make capitalism a success because capitalism enriches New York's elites at the expense of its downtrodden?

In Hungary and Czechoslovakia party politburos suddenly fall like dominoes, proving once again that authoritarianism is a crime against humanity. But is capitalism thereby a success because its politicians enter office in electoral charades and then leave to go to jail or become CEOs?

The overwhelmingly popular peaceful revolutions in Poland and East Germany reconfirm the utter bankruptcy of their post World War II social orders. But does this make poverty, ecological decay, and alienation in the U.S. desirable because it continues without major opposition? Was the Soviet economy desirable before the opposition developed its present strength?

Current events—like events every day for the past century—put a pox on both these houses. But since neither house has been based on an egalitarian, participatory foundation, current events do not discredit hope.

## Socialism Repudiated?

The Heilbronian argument goes that since Soviet, Chinese, and Eastern European leaders all called their countries "socialist," and since Henry Kissinger called them "socialist," and since the *New York Times* called them "socialist," and since Heilbroner and nearly all Western Marxists called them "socialist," these countries must have had economies embodying socialist principles. The crises of these economies therefore indicate that socialist values—the only alternative to capitalist values—are repudiated.

This would ring true if the label "socialist" applied, but Soviet, Chinese, and Eastern European leaders lied when they called their economies socialist. Henry Kissinger and the *New York Times* lied about this as well, and Western Marxists like Heilbroner have been either deceived, foolish, or also lying. Socialist values —assuming that by this we mean *egalitarian and participatory* values—have never characterized any of these countries. People who fled East Germany in the Winter of 1989 had *never* experienced egalitarianism, so how could they be rejecting it? Workers in Poland have never managed their own economic lives, so how can their bankrupt economy prove that if workers did manage their own lives everything would fall apart?

Whatever you decide to call the economies of the Soviet Union, China, and Eastern Europe—we prefer the term "coordinatorism"—it is critical to realize that they are not now and never have been egalitarian and participatory. If we don't realize that, we cannot understand the roots of their current crisis or alternative possibilities. Worse yet, we may mistakenly conclude that the

*"Whatever you decide to call them—we prefer the term "coordinatorism"— it is critical to realize that the economies in the Soviet Union, China, and Eastern Europe are not now and never have been egalitarian and participatory."*

—3

problems in the East stemmed from trying to be too egalitarian and participatory.

Certainly the Eastern bloc countries eliminated private ownership of the means of production and thereby rejected capitalism. But even beyond the political atrocity that was Stalinism, these countries only replaced capitalist management with bureaucratic management. Instead of developing democratic procedures by which workers and consumers could plan their joint endeavors efficiently and fairly, the new rulers imposed hierarchical planning that excluded ordinary workers and consumers alike from participating in economic decision making. As a result, they traded one ruling class, the capitalists, (ring out the old boss) for another, which we call the coordinators (ring in the new).

In these economies a ruling class of coordinators monopolized decision making, higher education, and material perks. Ordinary workers had little if anything to say about what they produced and how they produced it. About this system an eminent Soviet economist, Nikolai Shemelev, recently wrote (*Dissent*, Fall 1989): "Massive apathy, indifference, theft, and disrespect for honest work... have led to the virtual physical degradation of a significant part of the people as a result of alcoholism and idleness. There is a lack of belief in the officially announced objectives and purposes, in the very possibility of a more rational organization of social and economic life..." The economy in the Soviet Union is a mess *and always has been.* But even ignoring the fact that Shemelev's description sounds like downtown Milwaukee, Boston, San Francisco, and Miami, Shemelev's indictment tells us only that centrally planned coordinatorism has unraveled. It says nothing about egalitarianism and participation, because these values were long since abandoned and Soviet institutions preclude their attainment.

If you believe that Soviet working people have until now controlled their own assembly lines, decided their own product designs, and determined who gets to eat the wheat they grow and be warmed by the coal they mine, the current turmoil should leave you, like Heilbroner, feeling that people are creatures of such decrepit design that an economy based on competition and hierarchical control is the only antidote to intrinsic human sloth and inefficiency. If you believe the Soviet Union has been socialist, then current evidence would indicate that workers in power create not classlessness, but a mess. However, if you adopt the Heilbronian view, as we will show, you embrace cynicism unnecessarily because in the countries whose economies are now "failing," workers have never had power. A better economy for them *and* us remains a real possibility.

*"As a result, they traded one ruling class, the capitalists, (ring out the old boss) for another, which we call the coordinators (ring in the new)."*

*"A better economy for them and us remains a real possibility."*

## Coordinatorism

Following the fine and sober book by the Hungarians George Konrad and Ivan Szelenyi, *The Intellectuals on the Road to Class Power* (Harcourt Brace Jovanovich), we can transcend the

U.S. government, the Soviet government, the *New York Times*, and most Western Marxists to see that in the Eastern bloc workers do not and *never have* ruled their own economic lives. There, as in the West, intellectuals' earnings are considerably higher than workers' earnings. White-collar conceptual workers live in larger, more comfortable dwellings in better neighborhoods. They get quicker permission to settle in the cities and to inhabit subsidized housing with superior services. They live relatively close to their places of work, while a good part of the working class is obliged to commute from ill-serviced villages or suburban ghettos. Children of the intelligentsia go to better schools and attain university degrees in higher proportion. Only intellectuals and their dependents gain entry to special hospitals providing outstanding care for state and party officials. Even the cafeterias of institutions employing mostly intellectuals offer better meals than factory canteens.

More important, Konrad and Szelenyi also tell us that, "for all his [sic] alleged 'leading role,' [the worker in these economies] has just as little say in the high- or low-level decisions of his enterprise as the worker in a capitalist plant. He has no voice in deciding whether operations will be expanded or cut back, what will be produced, what kind of equipment he will use and what direction (if any) technical development will take, whether he will work for piece rates or receive an hourly wage, how performance will be measured and production norms calculated, how workers' wages will evolve relative to the profitability of the enterprise, or how the authority structure of the plant, from managing director to shop foreman, will operate." Workers, then, get what they can the same way in the East as in the West—by demanding and occasionally winning it—here from capitalists, there from coordinators.

In capitalism, capitalists own the means of production, use markets for allocation, define the purpose and character of work, and hire and fire workers (*and* managers). In coordinatorism, capitalists are gone. Managers, planners, engineers, and other intellectuals define work, using either central planning or markets for allocation. Workers continue to carry out tasks defined by others.

While their class structures and internal dynamics yield different allocations of wealth and income, in one respect these two systems closely resemble each other: "labor is external to the worker." Ironically, these words that Marx wrote to describe capitalism apply as well to coordinatorism. "Workers do not affirm themselves in their work. They do not feel content but unhappy." Work does not "freely develop workers' physical and mental energies" but "mortifies their body and ruins their minds." Workers "only feel themselves outside their work, and in their work feel outside themselves." They are "at home when they are not working and when they are working they are not at home." "Workers' labor is therefore not voluntary but coerced; it is forced labor." It is "not the satisfaction of a need; it is merely a means to satisfy needs external to it." The contest between the U.S. and the Soviet economic systems has always been largely irrelevant for workers since neither system serves them and both oppress them.

# Coordinatorism

*"In coordinatorism, capitalists are gone. Managers, planners, engineers, and other intellectuals define work, using either central planning or markets for allocation. Workers continue to carry out tasks defined by others."*

For those readers interested in our critique of Marxist theory, see our *Unorthodox Marxism* and *Marxism and Socialist Theory* (both published by South End Press, 1978, 1981). For a more detailed critique of the Soviet, Chinese, and Cuban experiences, see our *Socialism Today and Tomorrow* (South End Press, 1981). For a more detailed description of our alternative approach to understanding history and society, an approach emphasizing economics, gender, culture, and politics on an equal, interactive footing, see *Liberating Theory*, coauthored with Noam Chomsky, Leslie Cagan, Mel King, Lydia Sargent, and Holly Sklar (South End Press, 1986). Finally, for those interested in a more mathematical presentation of arguments regarding the inherent deficiencies of coordinator and capitalist economies, see our *Quiet Revolution in Welfare Economics* (Princeton University Press, 1990).

*Liberating Theory*

by
Michael Albert
Leslie Cagan
Noam Chomsky
Robin Hahnel
Mel King
Lydia Sargent
Holly Sklar

*"So the choices for modern economic institutions are threefold—capitalism, coordinatorism, or what we call 'participatory economics.' The failure of coordinatorism doesn't imply that the only remaining option is capitalism."*

So whose "needs external to it" *do* govern work in coordinator economies? Konrad and Szelenyi don't hedge: "The Communist parties, after coming to power, quickly dissolved or transformed every organization in which only workers participated, from workers' councils, factory committees, and trade unions, to workers' singing societies, theatrical groups, and sports clubs...." From this Konrad and Szelenyi deduce that Bolshevism "offered the intellectuals a program for freeing themselves of the duty of representing particular interests once power had been secured, and it used particular interests simply as a means of acquiring power." They conclude that "with the expropriation of the expropriators— that is, with the transfer of the right to dispose over the surplus product from landlords and capitalists to intellectuals in power, or to worker cadres whose political positions and functions made intellectuals of them—and with the destruction of the immediate producers' organs of management and control—the Bolsheviks traced the outlines of a new rational-redistributive system [i.e. coordinatorism]."

Coordinatorism distributes productive responsibilities so that some people (the coordinators) do primarily conceptual, administrative, and creative tasks, while others (the workers) do primarily rote tasks defined by others; that is, the former rule the latter. But the promise of economic liberation has always been to distribute productive responsibilities so that *everyone* has a fair share of opportunities for performing conceptual and executionary labor with all workers thereby entitled and prepared to play a proportionate role in determining events. This is a "third way."

So the choices for modern economic institutions are *threefold—* capitalism, coordinatorism, and what we call "participatory economics." The failure of coordinatorism doesn't imply that the only remaining option is capitalism.

For readers versed in the relevant history, it is instructive to remember what Karl Marx said about desirable economies in his *Philosophic Manuscripts*: "In the individual expression of my own life I would have brought about the immediate expression of your life, and so in my individual activity I would have directly confirmed and realized my authentic nature, my human, communal nature.... My labor would be the free expression and hence the enjoyment of life." This sentiment was and is liberating. But it has *nothing* in common with regimented central planning, the competitive selfishness of markets, or the authoritarian sentiments of official Marxism itself. Therefore the failure of these systems says nothing about the efficacy of trying to make our labors "the free expression and hence the enjoyment of life."

## The Origins of Coordinatorism

So where did coordinatorism begin? Few commentators today have anything nice to say about Stalin, but the problems of

Eastern bloc coordinatorism and political authoritarianism began much earlier. In other writings, listed on page 6, we have traced contemporary difficulties back to weaknesses in the original Marxist theoretical framework. Here we illustrate the anti-egalitarian and antiparticipatory sentiments of the leaders of the Russian revolution.

Leon Trotsky, a famous creator of the first coordinator economic system, said that the social rule of workers over society "is expressed...not at all in the form in which individual economic enterprises are administered." That is, Trotsky felt it would be fine for the Bolsheviks to leave the usual factory hierarchy in place so long as central administrators like himself ruled "in the interests of workers." As to why Trotsky championed "one-man management" in the factory we need look no further than his cynical view of human nature: "It is a general rule that man will try to get out of work. Man is a lazy animal." Naturally comrades at the center of society must sometimes coerce "lazy animals" for their own good. Finally, Trotsky added: "I consider that if the Civil War had not plundered our economic organs of all that was strongest, most independent, most endowed with initiative, we should undoubtedly have entered the path of one-man management much sooner and much less painfully." In other words, Trotsky didn't reluctantly accede to coordinator structures out of necessities compelled by the Civil War, as apologists maintain, but because he preferred them. These elitist sentiments defined Trotsky's agenda for society, a coordinator and not socialist agenda in which central administrators would appoint "one-man managers" who would rule over "lazy workers," in the workers' own interests, of course. If autonomous workers' organizations must be smashed in the process, so be it. They only prevent those such as Trotsky from protecting workers from the consequences of their own laziness—from ruling the workers to free them, so to speak. It is clear this coordinator agenda had nothing to do with making labor a "free expression and hence the enjoyment of life."

Lenin evidenced his own coordinator orientation when he argued: "It is absolutely essential that all authority in the factories should be concentrated in the hands of management." He followed this logic to its conclusion, noting that "any direct intervention by the trade unions in the management of enterprises must be regarded as positively harmful and impermissible." Whereas Trotsky appealed to a cynical view of human nature to justify coordinatorism, Lenin appealed to another bulwark of antidemocratic economic ideology, modern technology. "Large scale machine industry which is the central productive source and foundation of socialism calls for absolute and strict unity of will... How can strict unity of will be ensured? By thousands subordinating their will to the will of one." Apparently for Lenin, like Trotsky, it was sufficient that the "will of one" be well motivated, an analysis Stalin no doubt appreciated.

Between revolutionary dictatorship and the state principle the difference is only in the external situation. In substance both are one and the same: the ruling of the majority by the minority in the name of the alleged stupidity of the first and the alleged superior intelligence of the second. Therefore both are equally reactionary, both having as their result the invariable consolidation of the political and economic privileges of the ruling minority and the political and economic enslavement of the masses of people.

—Mikhail Bakunin
*Statism and Anarchism*

*"In other words, Trotsky didn't reluctantly accede to coordinator structures out of Civil War-compelled necessity, as apologists maintain, but because he preferred them."*

*"Apparently for Lenin, like Trotsky, it was sufficient that the 'will of one' be well motivated, an analysis Stalin no doubt appreciated."*

In response to workers who didn't accept his self-serving analysis and demanded more say over economic policy, Lenin thundered: "A producer's congress! What precisely does that mean? It is difficult to find words to describe this folly. I keep asking myself can they be joking? Can one really take these people seriously? While production is always necessary, democracy is not. Democracy of production engenders a series of radically false ideas." Perhaps one of the radically false ideas Lenin had in mind was that work should be "the free expression and hence the enjoyment of life."

In contrast to the coordinator sentiments of Lenin and Trotsky, Rosa Luxemburg expressed a liberatory disposition when she criticized the Bolsheviks: "Finally we saw the birth of a far more legitimate offspring of the historical process: the Russian workers' movement, which for the first time, gave expression to the real will of the popular masses. Then the leadership of the Russian revolution leapt up to balance on their shoulders, and once more appointed itself the all powerful director of history, this time in the person of his highness the Central Committee of the Social Democratic Workers Party. This skillful acrobat did not even realize that the only one capable of playing the part of director is the collective ego of the working class, which has sovereign right to make mistakes and to learn the dialectics of history by itself. Let us put it quite bluntly: the errors committed by a truly revolutionary workers' movement are historically far more fruitful than the correct decisions of the finest Central Committee."

Luxemburg captured the difference between coordinator and liberatory inclinations when she said: "The discipline which Lenin has in mind is driven home to the proletariat not only in the factory, but in the barracks, and by all sorts of bureaucracies, in short by the whole power machine of the centralized bourgeois state… It is an abuse of words to apply the same term 'discipline' to such unrelated concepts as the mindless reflex motions of a body with a thousand hands and a thousand legs, and the spontaneous coordination of the conscious political acts of a group of men. What can the well-ordered docility of the former have in common with the aspirations of a class struggling for its emancipation?"

The answer, of course, is nothing. The question that remains is whether we can create an economic system that is efficient, equitable, and ecologically sound based on the self-organization and collective self-management of workers and consumers.

## The Big Lie

Explaining the Orwellian semantics of the Heilbronian understanding of the twentieth century, Noam Chomsky tells us in *Language and Politics* (Black Rose Books) that since the Bolshevik revolution, "both of the major world propaganda systems have described this destruction of socialist elements as a victory of socialism. For western capitalism, the purpose is to defame socialism by associating it with Moscow's tyranny; for the Bolsheviks, the purpose was to gain legitimacy by appealing to the goals of authentic socialism." In line with our own analysis, Chomsky also notes that "particularly since 1917, Marxism—or more accurately, Marxism-Leninism—has become, as Bakunin predicted, the ideology of a 'new class' of revolutionary intelligentsia who exploit popular revolutionary struggles to seize state power. They proceed to impose a harsh and authoritarian rule to destroy socialist institutions, as Lenin and Trotsky destroyed the factory councils and soviets. They will also do what they can to undermine and destroy moves toward authentic socialism elsewhere, if only because of the ideological threat." Moreover, he adds, "this two-pronged ideological assault, combined with other devices available to those with real power, has dealt a severe blow to libertarian socialist currents that once had considerable vitality, though the popular commitments to such ideals constantly reveal themselves in many ways."

But to rebut the "two-pronged assault," in the same volume Chomsky tells an interviewer that "My own hopes and intuitions are that self-fulfilling and creative work is a fundamental human need, and that the pleasures of a challenge met, work well done, the exercise of skill and craftsmanship, are real and significant, and are an essential part of a full and meaningful life. The same is true of the opportunity to understand and enjoy the achievements of others, which often go beyond what we ourselves can do, and to work constructively in cooperation with others…. The task for a modern

All who are not lunatics are agreed about certain things. That it is better to be alive than dead, better to be adequately fed than starved, better to be free than a slave. Many people desire those things only for themselves and their friends; they are quite content that their enemies should suffer. These people can be refuted by science: Humankind has become so much one family that we cannot insure our own prosperity except by insuring that of everyone else. If you wish to be happy yourself, you must resign yourself to seeing others also happy.
—Bertrand Russell
*The Science to Save Us From Science*

industrial society is to achieve what is now technically realizable, namely a society which is really based on free voluntary participation of people who produce and create, live their lives freely within institutions they control, and with limited hierarchical structures, possibly none at all."

And that is our purpose in this book. Not merely to help people understand the U.S. economy. Not to change it to a different form of class rule. But to help make it classless by reorganizing production, consumption, and allocation to elevate social solidarity, collective self-management, and productive diversity to the highest priority, reducing hierarchical structures until there are "possibly none at all."

To consign egalitarian and participatory sentiments to the ashcan of history on the grounds that the coordinator economies of the East have crumbled under the dead weight of their own authoritianism, inequity, and hypocrisy is a convenient nonsequitor for champions of capitalism. In the East people are currently seeking liberty. We should hope they are not sidetracked by Twinkies, Toyotas, and the manipulations of their leaders, eager to enjoy the even greater advantages that capitalism offers *them*. While the economic vision put forward in this book is motivated by activism in the United States, we think it is equally relevant and perhaps more timely for dissidents to the East, and, for that matter, to the South.

*—Michael Albert and Robin Hahnel*
*December 1990*

# Introduction

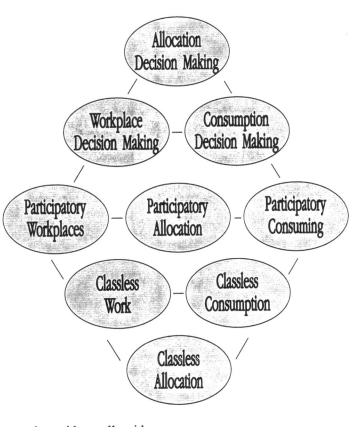

*An important scientific innovation rarely makes its way by gradually winning over and converting its opponents: it rarely happens that Saul becomes Paul. What does happen is that its opponents gradually die out and that the growing generation is familiarized with the idea from the beginning.*

—Max Planck

Capitalism institutionalizes inequality, promotes poverty, wages war, and denies dignity. It champions competition, eviscerates ecologies, and provides malls with miles of aisles—some for Moneybags, others for the average consumer. Eastern bloc economies reduced inequality but also deadened, decayed, and dissolved. Moreover, they offered no malls for anyone. Can an alternative new economy yield consumer satisfaction *and* equity, variety, solidarity, and self-management?

The generally accepted answer is "no, we must accept Western or Eastern economic models, tempering their ill effects via clever reforms." The effect of the resulting cynicism on popular aspirations was best described by an Italian scholar-activist, Antonio Gramsci, who said: "Indifference is the dead weight of history. It is a lead ball to the innovator, it is the inert matter which drowns the most sparkling enthusiasms, it is the swamp which surrounds the old city and defends it better than the most solid walls, better than the bodies of its soldiers, because it swallows the assailants in its slimy mires, it decimates them, disheartens them and, at times, makes them desist from their heroic undertaking."

Economic pundits claim that hierarchy, inequality, and markets or central planning are inevitable. We claim these are myths that only serve economic elites. We believe that, contrary to popular opinion, people can quite effectively manage their own economic affairs, and that they can do so equitably, humanely, *and* efficiently. To aim for endless abundance or for saintly behavior is "utopian" in the negative sense, and is not our purpose. But to think about how an economy can promote rather than subvert participatory, egalitarian goals is "utopian" in the positive sense that recognizes

*"Economic pundits claim that hierarchy, inequality, and markets or central planning are inevitable. We claim these are myths that only serve economic elites."*

Wonder each morning how you're going to hold on till evening, each Monday how you'll make it to Saturday. Reach home without the strength to do anything but watch TV, telling yourself you'll surely die an idiot...Long to smash everything... once a day, feel sick...because you've traded your life for a living; fear that the rage mounting within you will die down in the end, that in the final analysis people are right when they say: "an, you can get used to anything."
—Andre Gorz
*Capitalism in Crisis in Everyday Life*

that to have no goals is to passively accept an "old city" that squanders our potentials.

We live in the richest country in the world. It is tied for 31st, with Albania, in infants with low birth weight and 211 children die each week from malnutrition and poor care. We live in the richest country in the world and so do over 31 million poor people, 3 million of whom are homeless and wander the streets eating garbage-can dinners and sleeping in alleys. Why this pain amidst riches? In part because the top one-half of 1 percent of U.S. citizens hold about one-third of all U.S. wealth.

We live in the richest country in the world. One out of four children under six years of age are growing up poor, including 40 percent of all Latino children and 50 percent of all Black children. Violent crime is up 37 percent in the past decade, one person in twenty suffers some sort of burglary, assault, rape, or murder each year, there are 250 reported rapes daily, one every 6 minutes, and a woman is beaten every 19 seconds. We live in the richest country in the world. The mortality rate for black infants is twice that for whites and there is 1 successful suicide every 20 minutes with over ten times that number of failed attempts. Why this crime and despair amidst riches? In part because in 1988 the average chief executive officer of a U.S. corporation earned as much as 93 factory workers or 72 teachers. We live in the richest country in the world but capitalist success triumphs only in boardrooms and mansions.

In countries outside our immediate borders where our influence is greatest, Central America, of the 850,000 children born yearly 100,000 will die before the age of 5 from preventable disease and malnutrition because their resources are used to benefit our elites.

Depending on the type of economy a society has, work can build or erode confidence, consumption can fulfill needs or feed alienated habits, economic decision making can incorporate or exclude participation, and allocation can enrich the few by impoverishing the many or generate equality for all. Can't we agree that it would be desirable to transform our economy so that every citizen can lead a dignified, fullfilling life, employing their capacities as they prefer and enjoying society's offerings equally? Can't we agree that it would be desirable to transform our economy so that we respect others and are respected by them, all sharing in decisionmaking? Can't we agree that it would be desirable to overcome alienation, inequality, and the war of each against all, and to transform our economy so young people face the future with eagerness instead of resignation, so we do not destroy the planet, and so hierarchical structures are reduced until there are "possibly none at all"?

*"Can't we agree that it would be desirable to transform our economy so that every citizen can lead a dignified, fullfilling life, employing their capacities as they prefer, and enjoying society's offerings equally?"*

## Contents

In this book we decribe a new type of economy. In this new economy, work is carried out under the auspices of democratic workplace councils, one person one vote, with sensible delegation of responsibilities. There is no fixed workplace hierarchy. Each worker has a complex of responsibilities—some conceptual, some manual; some empowering, some rote—such that each worker's set of tasks (or "job complex") is balanced equitably with those of other workers. Each worker has a fair share of both desirable and not so desirable things to do, has comparable responsibilities and opportunities, and is equally prepared to participate in decision making.

Consumers receive roughly equal shares of the social product. While they still shop, act on impulse, and borrow and save, consumers must also do a reasonable job of predicting their consumption in advance. Changes in production and consumption eliminate needless waste in packaging, advertising, product duplication, etc. Collective goods are chosen by consumer councils with one person one vote. Equity and self management prevail, but so do respect for privacy and a positive attitude toward diversity and experimentation.

Participatory planning in the new economy is a means by which worker and consumer councils negotiate and revise their proposals for what they will produce and consume. All parties relay their proposals to one another via "facilitation boards." In light of each round's new information, workers and consumers revise their proposals in a way that finally yields a workable match between consumption requests and production proposals. The system rests on a comprehensive exchange of information including a new type of "indicative prices" to help with calculations, data about supply and demand to help people create proposals, and qualitative accounts of social relations to promote better decisions and greater solidarity.

The following 6 chapters deal with the norms and structure of workplaces (1 and 2), consumption (3 and 4), and allocation (5 and 6). Then chapters 7, 8, and 9 deal with the mechanisms of decision making from the perspective of work, consumption, and allocation respectively. Chapter 10 discusses the role of computers in a participatory economy, and the implications of our findings for strategy and transition are treated in chapter 11. A Glossary, beginning on page 151, includes brief definitions of original and technical terms used in the book.

While all this is logical and orderly, it places a heavy burden on readers who may have different opinions about what we should address first. Though *Looking Forward* addresses all important aspects of a new economy, we discuss production and consumption *before* allocation, and institutional structures *before* details of decision making procedures. For some readers questions will arise in early sections that are not addressed until later. We apologize, but no ordering could entirely avoid this inconvenience.

Throughout *Looking Forward* illustrations and graphics clarify points raised in the text. With only a few exceptions, these were conceived and produced by Matt Wuerker. At various points writ-

> The task for a modern industrial society is to achieve what is now technically realizable, namely, a society which is really based on free voluntary participation of people who produce and create, live their lives freely within institutions they control, and with limited hierarchical structures, possibly none at all.
>
> —Noam Chomsky
> *Language and Politics*

ten commentary appears in the margins. In most instances these are quotations meant to clarify or situate ideas in the text. When these appear in italics and with quotation marks, they are lifted directly from the main text. In all other instances their author is identified. Occasional sidebars in roman type provide factual information about relevant circumstances in the U.S.

Readers might be interested to know that a companion volume to *Looking Forward, The Political Economy of Participatory Economics* (Princeton University Press 1991), covers the same ground more abstractly, using arguments and mathematical demonstrations geared to economists. But anyone who reads this book will be able to follow the main line of argument in the companion volume.

# Work Without Hierarchy

*[We saw] a condition of society in which there should be neither rich nor poor, neither idle nor over-worked, neither brain-sick brain workers, nor heartsick hand workers, in a word, in which all men [sic] would be living in equality of condition and would manage their affairs unwastefully, and with the full consciousness that harm to one would mean harm to all—the realization at last of the meaning of the word common-wealth.*

—William Morris

NON-COMS, PRIVATES, and generals emerge in all known economies. Economists say this occurs because only a few people can make intelligent decisions, set policies, manage others, and develop new techniques, while most can only do what they are told. Few command. Most follow. Few shoulder responsibility. Most accept passivity. Is this God's will? Human nature? Or what?

## Human Labor

Assume a society with a school system that empowers every graduate to hold a responsible position. Some graduates are science buffs while others favor aesthetic involvement. Some are verbal, others more visual or mathematical. Some take pleasure in creative handiwork while others despair of manually assembling the simplest product. But despite this healthy diversity, if we accept that in this hypothetical example whatever their many differences *all* graduates preparing to enter the workforce have learned how to make responsible choices about social issues, then we can look at how, in any particular economy, this universal decision-making preparedness is enhanced or dissipated by the work people do.

In light of the above, if we can keep in mind the following three ideas about work, we will be well prepared to understand how work enhances or dissipates skills in different economies.

1. Work produces human qualities.

Inputs to work include tools, natural resources, products of others' labor, *and* workers' energies, skills, knowledge, and social relations. Outputs include commodities for consumption, unintended byproducts, *and* workers' altered moods, increased or diminished skills, and altered personalities. If work is rote, frustrating, and mindnumbing, it dampens skills and self-esteem. If work is complex and challenging, it enhances skills and self-esteem.

This means the jail keeper, assembly line worker, personnel manager, and accountant all owe elements of their personalities to the jobs they do. Likewise, the joy or fear, wisdom or foolishness that different workers have arise partly from the economic activities those workers undertake. Of course people are not solely determined by economic life, nor is economic life uninfluenced by extra-economic factors, but it should be evident that economies (as much as kinship, culture, and politics) affect not only what we can have and do, but also who we are and what we want.

2. The human qualities work produces in turn affect what responsibilities we can hold and what level of participation in decision making we can sustain.

Whether we are knowledgeable, skilled, energetic, or sociable affects our ability to succeed in work-related decision making. If we have these attributes we do better. What could be more obvious? If some of us do one kind of work (systems engineer) and others do another (receptionist), and if the two produce markedly different knowledge, skill, and/or dispositions, people doing the different jobs will have different likelihood of advancing up workplace job hierarchies. Indeed, when workers do not get their different abilities and inclinations from schooling or socialization, the only option left is that they get them from "on the job acculturation."

*"…all owe elements of their personalities to the jobs they do."*

3. Any economy that *produces class divisions* must differentiate among new workers building confidence and skill in some and generating apathy in others. In contrast, any economy that aspires to classlessness must welcome new workers into balanced jobs that develop confidence and skills in *all*.

Suppose a capable young work force enters industry only to exert little influence over boring work. Regardless of their initial abilities, suppose only a small percentage win promotions offering more knowledge, freer workdays, and greater time for study. We can confidently predict that each time these few climb the promotion ladder, their chances of falling back will decrease. Each step up will increase their skills and confidence. In contrast, workers left below will continue to follow orders and many of their potentials will atrophy for want of "exercise." This is a class division emerging from *the way work is organized.* Moreover, we all know that real-world economies sharply divide conceptual and executionary tasks in just this way, thereby fostering growing disparities between those who order and those who obey. Is it possible that organized differently, economies can integrate conceptual and executionary responsibilities to foster comparable skills for all actors and eliminate these divisions? How?

Thus council organization weaves a variegated net of collaborating bodies through society, regulating its life and progress according to their own free initiative. And all that in the councils is discussed and decided draws its actual power from the understanding, the will, the action of working humankind itself.
—Anton Pannekoek

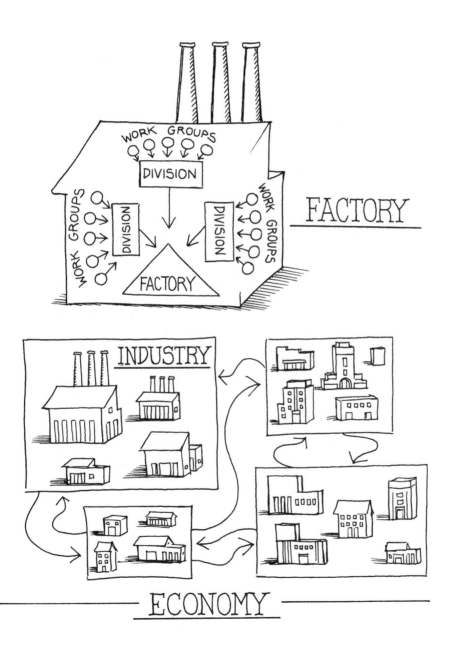

## Workplace Organization

Now, as to occupations, we shall clearly not be able to have the same division of labor in [our workplaces] as now: vicarious servanting, sewer-emptying, butchering, letter carrying, boot-blacking, hair-dressing, and the rest of it, will have come to an end; we shall either make all these occupations agreeable to ourselves in some mood... or we shall have to let them lapse altogether. A great many fidgety occupations will come to an end: we shan't put a pattern on a cloth or a twiddle on a jug-handle to sell it, but to make it prettier and to amuse ourselves and others.
—William Morris
*The Society of the Future*

Contemporary job definitions foster hierarchy. Can different job definitions combat hierarchy? Do we have to reject all divisions of labor if people are to have a commensurate say in decisions that affect them at work? Or can we reduce hierarchical structures until there are "possibly none at all" and yet retain a practical and efficient organization?

### Workers' Councils

One tool for eliminating workplace hierarchy is "workers' councils" of all relevant workers. Small councils deal with immediate problems confronting small work groups. Larger councils make decisions for work teams encompassing a network of work groups, for example, in a wing or on a floor. Still larger councils make decisions for a division, a complex of divisions, or a plant, and federations of councils make decisions for an industry. Every council and federation principally concerns itself with affairs at its own level while contributing to decisions at higher levels in proportion to how they are affected. Some decisions require a majority of all members. Others, where the change has more drastic implications, may require two-thirds. Nothing requires that every decision must await every council's or worker's input. Personnel decisions are made only by people directly concerned. Decisions about breaks that affect a whole floor would be made by all involved on that floor. Plant decisions would be made by plant councils.

But while necessary, formally democratic councils are not *sufficient* for promoting workplace participatory democracy. Even if sweepers have a council, representation in higher councils, and full voting rights in plant decisions, they will never exert the same influence as managers who develop budgets or design products. Despite equal rights, sweepers' boring work will not challenge their intellectual capacities or provide them with information about technological options or with skill at making decisions. Work-induced attributes will push them to follow rather than lead so that *even in democratic councils* people who hold jobs conferring greater knowledge of work functions, greater time for personal study, and greater self-confidence will dominate the decision making. We therefore need something more than councils to reduce hierarchy to "possibly none at all."

*"We therefore need something more than councils to reduce hierarchy to 'possibly none at all'."*

### Job Rotation

One approach sometimes offered to overcome job inequalities and the hierarchies they create is to rotate everyone through diverse tasks—the engineer ocassionally sweeps and so on. Can this succeed?

Rotation can create mutual understanding, but the engineer will inevitably view a temporary "janitorial" assignment differently than the person for whom sweeping is an occupation. Parading through the ghetto or slinking through the country club doesn't confer membership in either. Hierarchies of power will not be undone by temporary shuffling. Something more is needed.

Moreover, doing one's "alternative service" someplace *other* than where one does one's main work would further negate the benefit of rotation. Rotation outside one's workplace would leave the habits of mystification, deference, and authoritarianism in *each* particular workplace unchallenged. That my manager does a stint of manual labor every other weekend in his neighborhood nursery will not diminish class division between him and me in our shared workplace. Nor would it matter much if I kept books part-time for a nursery in *my* neighborhood. Moreover, the proportion of rote workers likely to excel at creative involvements at home given their work-induced state of fatigue, depression, and alienation is low. More likely, rote workers at home will prefer unwinding in ways that do not generate skills that will make their rote work still more difficult to endure. Becoming members of a democratic council while maintaining present job definitions wouldn't resolve these problems.

*"Parading through the ghetto or slinking through the country club doesn't confer membership in either."*

It follows that while rotation can introduce variety and enrich people's understanding, it isn't sufficient. Participatory production requires more than democratic councils plus simple rotation. What do we do each day? Do we do one rote *or* one conceptual task? Do we do a bunch of rote *or* a bunch of conceptual tasks? Or do we do a combination of rote *and* conceptual tasks so that everyone has a "job complex" roughly balanced vis-a-vis empowerment? The unavoidable conclusion is that only having *comparably* empowering work lives will ensure that everyone participating in a council has sufficient confidence, skill, knowledge, and energy to have equal opportunities to influence council outcomes. Like it or not, only balanced job complexes are compatible with reducing hierarchy till there is "possibly none at all."

## Participatory Job Complexes

Classlessness and real rather than merely formal workplace democracy *require* that each worker has a job complex composed of comparably fulfilling responsibilities. Forming comparable job complexes therefore *requires* that we evaluate each workplace's tasks and carefully combine them into diverse "job complexes" that are equally empowering. Of course this doesn't mean everyone must do everything; this would be inefficient and usually even impossible. It does mean, however, that the half dozen or so tasks that I regularly do must be roughly as empowering as the different half dozen or so tasks that you regularly do if we are to participate as equals in council decision making.

In the individual expression of my own life I would have brought about the immediate expression of your life, and so in my individual activity I would have directly confirmed and realized my authentic nature, my human, communal nature. Our productions would be as many mirrors from which our natures would shine forth. This relation would be mutual: what applies to me would also apply to you. My labor would be the free expression and hence the enjoyment of life.

—Karl Marx
*Grundrisse*

An earthly kingdom cannot exist without inequality of persons. Some must be free, some serfs, some rulers, some subjects.
—Martin Luther
Werke, *Vol XVIII*

How can a rational being be ennobled by anything that is not obtained by its own exertions?
—Mary Wollstonecraft
*A Vindication of the Rights of Women*

In most workplaces there are hundreds of basic tasks. One organizational option is to combine tasks with the *same qualitative characteristics* into homogenous jobs. Some workers take phone messages and keep records. Others do research and manage. Everyone does *one level* of task and many more people have rote than have creative assignments. This is the capitalist *and* the coordinator approach.

A better option is to combine tasks into job complexes each of which has a *mix of responsibilities* guaranteeing workers roughly comparable circumstances. Everyone does a unique bundle of things that add up to an *equitable* assignment. Instead of secretaries answering phones *and* taking dictation, some workers answer phones *and* do calculations while others take dictation *and* design products. This is the participatory approach.

Moreover, even beyond balancing *within* each workplace, we must also adjust for differences *between* workplaces. For example, those who work in coal mines and those who work at publishing houses are not likely to find their work equally desirable or empowering. If one plant's average job complex is less desirable or empowering, workers there should enrich their work package by spending time doing more fulfilling tasks elsewhere. If some other plant's average job complex is more desirable or empowering, workers there should spend time doing less fulfilling tasks elsewhere. "Workplace rotation" balances inequalities *between* plants, while balanced job-complexes within plants prevent in-plant class stratification.

In the transition to a participatory workplace, publishing house workers will be less likely to welcome equalization *between* workplaces than will coal miners—just as engineers and lawyers

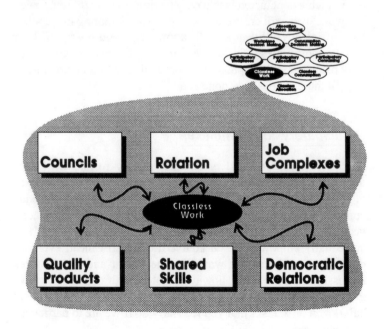

will be less likely than assembly workers and secretaries to agree that everyone can be trained to do a fair share of conceptual and executionary work *within* workplaces. Nonetheless, to attain participatory goals we must incorporate democratic councils, responsible rotation, *and* balanced job complexes within and across workplaces.

## Workplace Decision Making

One of the aims of participatory economics is for people to develop respect and concern for one another. To attain this type of solidarity, participatory workers must consider not only their own activities but what others must endure to prepare the materials they work on and what benefits their output will afford others. Democratic councils with balanced job complexes would help workers to operate according to such norms *so long as the rest of their economy also fosters such behavior*. Since neither markets nor central planning do, we naturally need to develop a new kind of participatory allocation to go with participatory production and consumption.

Unquestionably submission to the single will is absolutely necessary for the success of labor processes based on large scale machine industry....
Revolution demands, in the interests of socialism, that the masses unquestioningly obey the single will of the leaders of the labor process.

—Lenin

Studying this new allocation system (in chapters 5 and 6) will help answer many questions readers might already be asking, such as, who will work where, what they will be paid, etc. Still, it bears pointing out that switching to participatory allocation will also profoundly affect the content of work *in* each plant. For example, tricking people into buying things they don't need would make no sense once participatory allocation ensures that one's income doesn't depend on selling more goods. Indeed, relations among participatory production, consumption, and allocation ensure that to fully understand any one we must understand them *all*. Even familiar concepts like "manage," "job," "income," and "price" acquire a different meaning in participatory economies than in capitalism so that the general logic of the new economy will become clear only after all its features are explained. At this stage we claim only that to be participatory and equitable, an economy:

1. Must have democratic workplace councils.

2. Can benefit from efficacious use of job rotation.

3. Must have job complexes balanced for desirability and empowerment.

## Confronting Skeptics and Adversaries

Thus a ruling class emerges from the intellectual class to become the ultimate repository of the redistributive ethos and, as such, to give final sanction to all redistributive decisions.
—George Konrad and Ivan Szelenyi
*The Intellectuals on the Road to Class Power*

To run the above claims through a wringer of multi-faceted skepticism, we present a hypothetical dialogue between an advocate of participatory economics ("PE"), a proponent of

It is a general rule that man will try to get out of work. Man is a lazy animal.
—Trotsky

Largescale machine industry which is the central productive source and foundation of socialism calls for absolute and strict unity of will... How can strict unity of will be ensured? By thousands subordinating their will to the will of one.
—Lenin

A producer's congress! What precisely does that mean? It is difficult to find words to describe this folly. I keep asking myself can they be joking? Can one really take these people seriously? While production is always necessary, democracy is not. Democracy of production engenders a series of radically false ideas.
—Lenin

capitalism ("Cap"), an advocate of central planning ("Cent"), and a proponent of so-called "market socialism" ("Mark").

CAP: Your workplace is utopian. How does having everyone do everything increase productivity?

PE: I only said we should each do a variety of things that fully utilize our potentials...

CAP: It's ridiculous to expect passive people to be assertive. Pressuring them to do so will only create misery.

PE: If some people were genetically menial and others genetically conceptual you'd be right, but...

CAP: ...work affects us. So what? Capitalist jobs are hierarchical because they respect human nature, not because they stifle it. Bees don't create hierarchical hives against bee nature but because of it. Yes, capitalist work roles would create divisions even among a work force of identical human beings. But so what? There is no equal work force, just as there are no equal bees. Like bees, we have unequal jobs due to unequal natures.

CENT: I agree people inevitably excel in different areas but we shouldn't glorify one kind of contribution. The problem in capitalism is that working with one's head is considered more important than working with one's hands. But divisions on conceptual lines are just as natural as some people preferring art and others sports. We should divide work so society best utilizes people's special talents.

PE: Cent says some people are *innately* more conceptual and others more manual. But that means she thinks people are innately disposed to order or be ordered. To add that all kinds of work should be valued equally is an improvement but doesn't solve one problem. What conceptualizers get from their work will give them ever growing dispositions to lead. Conceptualizers will rule and hosannas to the merits of manual labor won't change this.

MARK: Of course everyone should pursue their own capabilities, but PE, why urge such a cumbersome model when markets work fine? Let workers organize their tasks however they prefer. But let the marketplace discipline their choices to make sure they are socially useful.

PE: Which sounds like my suggestion that workers' councils rate tasks and create job complexes. But I want them to do this in a different setting. Mark, your markets so constrain workers' options that their only sensible decision is to divide work in traditional ways...

MARK: That's nonsense...

PE: Is it? Operating in a market means submitting to the profit criterion. However much workers might want to employ social criteria, to ignore profitability would cause their firms to go belly-up. So, of course workers in market environments will hire others to count pennies for them. Counting pennies is what markets require, not what workers would prefer in a humane setting. Cap reveals the basis of all your attitudes when he admits that unequal outcomes don't bother him.

CAP: Yep.

PE: I can't prove we are all biologically capable of participating in decision making. But you can't prove that our significant differences are biologically rather than socially produced. Why not see what it what it would be like to develop everyone's participatory capacities? After all, it's our only hope for a humane society.

CAP: But it is ridiculous to assume we are all innately the same...

PE: ...not "the same," just all quite able to participate in making decisions and managing our lives...

CAP: ...you have to admit that if we allow people to specialize some will become better than others at managing. Rewarding them for a job well done will benefit those at the bottom because it is more efficient. It's so simple. Everyone understands it. Why are you so dense? Why not admit that some people manage better and some don't care? Even if we all have the ability to make decisions, some have more ability and work harder. Reward them and we'll all benefit.

CENT: I agree with Cap. Why allow everyone to participate? To serve an impossible dream, allowing all to participate in making decisions about complex issues would cripple planners' abilities to coordinate outcomes efficiently. Even if participation could be enhanced, why bother? Why not let those best suited to decision making do it? Why not let professional decision makers have the final say based on greater education and intelligence but directed toward the social good by political experts? You say you're not trying to level everyone down, PE, but that's what your system would do whether you recognize it or not.

MARK: Let the councils decide! If councils want everyone to vote, fine. If councils appoint experts to make decisions, fine. Let workers choose.

PE: Sure, let workers decide so long as we *impose* a market that insures that workers will hire you and your friends to run their workplaces. Mark, you conveniently ignore that markets create conditions that compel workers to decide things which would not be in their interest if they could eliminate markets.

And Cent, you don't want capitalists but you do want bosses. You throw a sop to workers' pride by praising their efforts. But you neglect to tell them that you also think your job is more important and you think you deserve better housing, more vacations, a nice car, and better schooling for your children. Cap makes your point more honestly. Why not maximize output by letting some people specialize in management and rewarding those who excel with power and wealth...

That which we at present call laziness is, rather, the disgust which men [sic] feel over breaking their backs for beggars' salaries and being, moreover, looked down upon and depreciated by the class which exploits them—while those who do nothing useful live like princes and are deferred to and respected by all.
—Ricardo Flores Magon
*Regeneracion*

I refuse to accept the idea that the 'isness' of man's present nature makes him morally incapable of reaching up for the 'oughtness' that forever confronts him.
—Martin Luther King, Jr.
*Nobel Prize Speech*

CAP: Exactly.

PE: My answer is that making economic decisions is not like swimming, running, or answering quiz questions. There is no winner in the race to make decisions, nor only one right answer to economic questions. Instead, the best economic answers nearly always involve merging the wisdom of diverse perspectives and implementing more than one policy to compare results. Moreover, participation wouldn't be a waste even if it didn't always yield better decisions because it pays off in workers' increased knowledge, confidence, solidarity, and fulfillment. I'm not saying you always have to maximize the number of voices heard. But we should create channels that allow all voices to express themselves with power and conviction.

'Incapacity of the masses.' What a tool for all exploiters and dominators, past, present, and future, and especially for the modern aspiring enslavers, whatever their insignia—Nazism, Bolshevism, Fascism, or Communism. 'Incapacity of the masses.' This is a point on which the reactionaries of all colors are in perfect agreement with the 'communists.' And this agreement is exceedingly significant.
—Voline
*The Unknown Revolution*

CAP: You're incorrigibly romantic. Job balancing would just waste time. Workers can't get equal benefits from doing different activities any more than everyone can benefit equally from listening to a Mahler symphony. Some people are too dumb to be more than a receptionist. You think people will work harder to make others happy. Where do you get such ideas?

CENT: Rotation can build respect for what others do. But we shouldn't destroy lines of authority or waste talent. And we shouldn't forget that some people enjoy being just receptionists. PE is right that workers can be motivated by more than greed, but material incentives are always going to matter most.

MARK: Right. Some people will choose to be receptionists. We should let people work at whatever they want, for whatever reasons.

PE: Yes, Cap, musically trained people will get more out of Mahler than you or I. But while everyone needn't learn everything, we all need to learn how to make plans, coordinate activities, and weigh alternatives. We won't all do these things equally well, but we will all do them well enough to bring our own particular experiences and insights to bear on decision making, especially regarding our own circumstances, which *we* do inevitably know best. Even you think everyone should learn to read despite the undeniable fact that some will do it faster and with more comprehension. I want the same for conceptual work and decision-making, that's all.

People get different pleasure from many important things because they have slightly different dispositions or prepare differently or even have different capacities. But for sex or sports we don't say that only the "best" should participate. That should be true for using one's head too.

CAP: But letting everybody participate in sports isn't the same as letting everyone play in the big leagues. And that's what you're suggesting when you say everyone should participate in important economic decisions.

PE: I just answered that when I said decisions are not like races. Expert results require participation of all concerned. And I never claimed people shouldn't be trained in and practice to get better at economic decisionmaking. Creating balanced job complexes is fair, humane, and productive. Other than people who are truly disabled, everyone is obviously capable of more than answering phones and taking messages. The myth that most people are incapable of intelligent participation no matter what training they get rationalizes an economic structure that forces most people to fill debilitating roles so others can rule.

Sure, Cent, people can get pleasure out of doing just about any job well. You might even learn to enjoy real work. But no one enjoys doing the same rote tasks over and over with no say and no opportunity to diversify. It doesn't matter how much you patronize their contribution.

And Mark, of course some people will choose to be a receptionist in today's economies. But you can't believe that if we had an effective school system and climate of equality anyone would opt to sit and take messages for you all day instead of having a diversified work complex. Would you choose to be a receptionist for crummy wages? For your current wages? Even for a substantial raise?

MARK: How substantial?

PE: The issue isn't only that everyone should have conceptual elements in his or her job complex. Your fear is no doubt that I am saying that even the greatest scientist or musician should do some manual work to balance his or her job complex. And you are right, I am saying exactly that.

CENT: See I told you so.

CENT: You're right, he's out of his mind.

PE: No I'm not. The scientist struggling to find a cure for cancer, the doctor able to perform the most delicate operations, or the author able to write the most uplifting novels are extreme cases. The real issue is most workers, not a few exceptional talents. But I do believe that the argument applies even to the most extreme cases. For by adopting the principle that everyone does a balanced complex we tap an important human potential in the great majority that would otherwise lie dormant if they only did rote work. Moreover, by creating respectful, egalitarian environments, we reduce the waste associated with elites trying to defend their position. The time that goes into class warfare can be enormous, and even the most exceptional scientist may benefit from a more egalitarian environment. Her total scientific contribution may increase even if some time that might have gone to research goes to less creative labors so long as time and emotional energy that now goes into defending status and dealing with bureaucracies no longer has to. And if this isn't so for some genius, then society ccould choose to grant a special dispensation every so often. I myself would vote to sacrifice output for more important social value. Perhaps others would decide differently. Fine.

The discipline which Lenin has in mind is driven home to the proletariat not only in the factory, but in the barracks, and by all sorts of bureaucracies, in short by the whole power machine of the centralized bourgeois state... It is an abuse of words to apply the same term 'discipline' to such unrelated concepts as the mindless reflex motions of a body with a thousand hands and a thousand legs, and the spontaneous coordination of the conscious political acts of a group of men. What can the well-ordered docility of the former have in common with the aspirations of a class struggling for its emancipation?
—Rosa Luxemburg

But it's getting late. We ought to quit. We'll have time to talk more about motivation after you let me describe participatory allocation where the broader implications of these choices become clearer.

# —2—

# Participatory Workplaces

*So you see, I claim that work in a duly ordered community should be made attractive by the consciousness of usefulness, by its being carried on with intelligent interest, by variety, and by its being exercised amidst pleasurable surroundings.*

—William Morris

In this chapter we will compare a few hypothetical participatory workplaces with capitalist and coordinator alternatives to clarify points made last chapter. In real participatory workplaces many workers may choose to structure their work differently than we describe in this chapter. Naturally, future workers will find countless acceptable ways to meet participatory norms depending on their circumstances, tastes, and local conditions. The options presented here are possibilities, not recipes that must be followed.

## Book Publishing

How would workers in a book publishing enterprise define and assign tasks? What would their worklife be like? Publishing always involves editorial, production, and accounting work, each including tasks ranging from rote to conceptual and repetitive to diverse. But workers can organize and carry out these tasks in different ways.

### Capitalist Publishing

The criteria capitalist publishing uses to determine how to combine diverse tasks into job complexes are profitability and maintaining hierarchies. Each book is a commodity to be sold for maximum revenue and produced at minimum cost. Whether people read the book is incidental. Given the option, most publishers will limit the range of offerings till the public learns to accept easily digested pablum.

Capitalist budgeting maximizes profits by holding off small creditors, taking advantage of beginning authors, and setting high prices for few offerings. Will consumers buy their how-to book or ours, their romance or ours, their 90-day diet fad or ours? Given society's race, class, political, and gender biases, what shibboleths must be observed? Given reviewers' attitudes, which books are likely to be discussed? Which should we give up for dead? To be sure, many enter the publishing field committed to promoting humane values. But the dynamics of the capitalist market require first one compromise, then another, until any humane values are totally lost under the bottom line of profits.

Jobs are defined, behavior patterns enforced, pay scales determined, and pink slips and promotions dispersed all to preserve hierarchy and best extract sufficient labor to keep business profitable. Employers "respect" prior attitudes of new employees so that social hierarchies born outside the firm reappear inside. Most women do what's considered "women's work." Most blacks do what's considered "blacks' work." Cleaning "girls," secretaries, receptionists, typesetters, and mailroom "boys" do the most deadening work for the lowest wages. Aside from other oppressive attributes, two bear special comment.

1. The broader creative powers of most workers steadily erode as most people work *down* to their assignments.

2. Everyone's emotional energies dissipate in efforts to rationalize and defend status and hierarchy.

The result is a waste of human resources, an immoral denial of most workers' capacities, and a reduction of publishing to producing commodities for a quick killing.

### Participatory Publishing: Northstart Press

Naturally, Northstart Press organizes jobs to accomplish tasks with dispatch at high quality. But Northstart's participatory priorities also require that all workers exercise their talents and express their wills.

Instead of selling books to make profits, Northstart's workers are pleased when readers are entertained or enlightened. Northstart workers choose among submissions by deciding whether readers will benefit sufficiently to merit the resources, time, and energy required to publish them.

Writing, editing, and design are done largely as now. But proofreading and copy-editing occur by computer program, formatting is automatic, and the result is stored in computer banks for electronic accessing. We can imagine that to save trees and other resources and to reduce onerous tasks most books *might* be electrically conveyed to portable booksize computers that have the heft, look, and feel of traditional books and allow readers to alter the size, layout, design, and resolution on their system's paper-page-like "screen." Only for volumes of special merit or on specific order would books be printed. In this way preparation and distribution costs could drop dramatically, scarce resources could be protected, and consumers could enjoy easy, direct, and nearly free access to whole libraries of information. Computer programs could also facilitate design by allowing easy manipulation of graphics, charts, and type style, size, and page alignment. Indeed, people's "electronic-books" might even allow them to choose larger type or more white space or even new pictures, graphs, or layout of their own design. While some of these technical changes could theoretically occur in a capitalist future, many will not because they would conflict with profitability and subvert hierarchy. While they could occur in a participatory economic future, whether they will will be determined in light of their human and social effects on work, consumption, libraries, bookstores, the ecology, and the reading experience. But these are issues of investment, a subject we will address in detail later.

Many business tasks would also differ in a participatory publishing house. Due to technological innovations (assuming they are adopted), most Northstart fulfillment—filling orders and tracking inventory—occurs by phone onto electronic books. Large warehouses are no longer necessary to store titles. Over production no longer leads to shredding unsold books. Fulfillment workers maintain records of people who access different titles since this information is useful to authors, researchers, and within Northstart.

We can summarize changes for other departments as well. The task of participatory promotion would be to help potential readers decide whether they want to take a closer look at titles, but there would be no effort to entice people to "buy" books they cannot benefit from. Participatory workers wouldn't want to waste resources, energy, or time producing inferior products. Northstart sends informative promotional messages to people most likely to enjoy, appreciate, or learn from new titles.

Similarly, the Northstart finance/budget department oversees scheduling within limits set by council decision-making. Finance/budget work differs from familiar capitalist norms in both data handling and data dissemination because what is valued alters. In a capitalist firm, data assembled by the finance/budget department is restricted so that top managers and owners have access, but no matter how many computer terminals exist, only a few employees can access this information. Were non-privileged workers able to access such information, they might use it to better gauge what wages to demand, or when they might best strike.

In contrast, at Northstart everyone works with any information they choose. Not only can those in promotion access budget data,

To get a a feel for the size of the U.S. economy that is to be made participatory note that in 1986 there were 68,076 agricultural services, forestry, and fishery establishments; 34,973 mining establishments; 355,452 manufacturing establishments; and 1,441,236 retail trade establishments. There were 937 metal mining establishments, 3,773 bituminous coal and lignite establishments, 23,322 oil and gas extraction establishments, 14,000 rubber and miscellanious plastic products establishments, 6,725 primary metal industries establishments, 17,374 electric and electronic equipment establishments, 6,152 textile mill product establishments, 57,299 printing and publishing establishments, 2,327 petroleum and coal product establishments, 187,430 food stores, 362,895 eating and drinking places, 36,037 general merchandise stores, 141,884 apparel and accessory stores, 205,597 real estate offices, 54,759 banks, 18,543 movie theaters, 2,018 museums, etc.

To get a feeling for the size of the U.S. economy in 1987 there were approximately 3.5 million salespeople, 1.7 million food servers, 1.4 million registered nurses, 2.7 million janitors and cleaners, 2.3 million general managers and top executives, 2.1 million cashiers, 2.2 million truck drivers, 2.3 million office clerks, 3.2 million secretaries.... The U.S. gross national product in 1988 was $4.8 trillion. Personal consumption was $3.2 trillion. Total government expenditures were just under $677 billion.

so can those in fulfillment, and people in fulfillment and promotion can access data from each other's departments as well. It won't be productive for everyone to analyze all data endlessly. But it will be desirable to organize information so every actor can understand Northstart's operations and experiment with projections.

### Job Complexes

What other changes might result from participatory organization? The most fundamental structural change is that each Northstart worker has a job complex including some editorial, production, and business responsibilities and encompassing roughly average positive and negative work attributes. The total array of tasks associated with producing play scripts, for example, is divided among a team so that each member has comparable tasks. Similarly, the editorial team working on novels allocates editing, working with authors, and soliciting new novels so that everyone gets to use their special talents and to fulfill their particular interests while no one enjoys all creative tasks or gets stuck with an excess of numbing tasks.

Instead of having head editors, copy editors, proofreaders, and secretaries, each editorial team includes equal members who have diverse responsibilities suited to their own tastes and talents but mindful of the need for equity. Though one person might do more copy-editing and another take more notes, what would be disallowed is allocating conceptual work entirely to one set of people and rote work entirely to another. The educational implications of this arrangement should be obvious. Education in a society with a participatory economy must provide its citizens with the skills, knowledge, and experience essential to playing a creative, self-managing role in society *and* in the special fields of their choice. The contrast to capitalism, where schools acclimate citizens to endure boredom and order-taking, should be obvious.

*"Education in a society with a participatory economy must provide its citizens the skills, knowledge, and experience essential to playing a creative, self-managing role in society and in the special fields of their choice."*

### Councils

Beyond equitable job definition, there would also be a council of all Northstart workers where each had equal voice and vote as well as smaller councils responsible for editing and producing fiction, general nonfiction, and technical books, and still smaller overlapping councils in each business division. A variety of teams would undertake preparing particular books or researching a particular reorganization of workplace technology. In assigning special jobs, there would be no need to make work the same for everybody at every moment. Equity would come on average—over reasonable spans of time—as when individuals get vacations at different times or spend months doing a time-consuming creative project and catch up on rote tasks later. One could even make provision that if a person "borrows" to take a vacation and then changes jobs, any "debt" incurred would hold over to the new workplace.

Northstart's yearly plan evolves through negotiations each May. Decisions are made about how many plays, novels, and books to accept and release during the year, and about work load, materials needed, work allocation, hiring new workers, and establishing new rules and technologies. Initial proposals come from all participants in the economy, go through a number of revisions, and finally "mesh" into a feasible plan, including a work plan for Northstart. Northstart budget and finance workers facilitate this "iterative" process at each stage by providing useful data and suggestions to all Northstart workers. No one expects everyone to have the same priorities. Nor is it assumed that everyone will agree that the final plan is necessarily the best possible one.

Northstart's proposals are altered from iteration to iteration by a process of give-and-take guided by information provided by other units. Finance/budget workers facilitate this updating, though it is overseen by the whole Northstart council. In any event, once a year's plan is determined, and we will understand this process better after addressing allocation in chapters 5 and 6, work for the new period begins.

As the year progresses, most decisions are taken within particular Northstart teams and councils, though some require ratification by the whole Northstart council, and others require approval of industry or consumer councils. But this does not mean that every decision is everyone's affair. Instead, decisions are made by those directly affected, and often people delegate authority and autonomy to others with whom they work. Participatory organization allows democracy without nosiness.

In a participatory workplace, of course there may be males and females, homosexuals and heterosexuals, blacks, whites, Asians, and Native Americans, Catholics, Protestants, Moslems, and Jews. But Northstart employees recognize that the cultural diversity that members of different social groups bring to work should be allowed to express itself in the context of job complexes balanced for empowerment and agreeableness. To help ensure this, every month optional caucus meetings discuss whether any workplace issues affect minority group interests. Workplace caucuses have autonomous rights to challenge arrangements they believe are sexually or racially oppressive. But since the rationale for these requirements *stems* not from a theory of economic relations but from theories of kinship and community relations, we do not treat the justification for employing such caucuses in further detail here (see lower sidebar on this page).

### Leadership

Notice that nothing in what we have described precludes exercising leadership. Production coordinators on particular books will exert influence over team members regarding quality and pace of work necessary to get the books completed. Finance-department decisions will be authoritative regarding budgeting. People work-

In considering the possibilities for a participatory economy in the U.S. it is important to remember that about a fourth of the federal governments' expenditures go directly to defense related purchases and staffing and that defense employment is about 1 million civilians plus about 2.1 million active duty military personnel. The U.S. defense budget in 1988 was just a bit over $290 billion. (In contrast, France spends about $28 billion, West Germany $28 billion, England $27 billion, Japan $20 billion, and Italy $13 billion.) Five of the largest corporations in the country, all received more than half their business from the federal government—Lockheed (86%), General Dynamics (85%), Martin Marietta (85%), McDonnell Douglas (65%), and Raytheon (55%). Retool much of this to address social needs, and the quality of life of the U.S. and much of the world could be vastly improved.

For a discussion of theoretical concerns and visionary aims relating to other spheres of social life than the economy which are, however, compatible with participatory economics, see *Liberating Theory* (South End Press), and the other books referenced on page 6. We return to this issue, as well, in the conclusion of this book.

Advertising is one of many wasteful sectors of the U.S. economy that can be greatly reduced. In 1988 $118 billion was spent on advertising in the U.S. (Philip Morris, Procter and Gamble, and GM combined for nearly $4 billion of it). In the top 20 we also find Pepsi, McDonald's, Ford, Anheuser-Busch, Nabisco, Kellogg, General Mills, Eastman Kodak, and Pillsbury. The 100 largest advertisers combined accounted for approximately $28 billion. Only a modest percentage of this would be required to finance the entire qualitative information apparatus of a participatory economy, with the rest of the savings going to improve the quality of life.

A society that gives to one class all the opportunities for leisure and to another all the burdens of work condemns both classes to spiritual sterility.
—Lewis Mumford

ing in personnel will exert leadership over disputes about job assignments. Editorial decisions will determine what is published.

Similarly, not having an editor-in-chief does not mean there will be no editor with final responsibility for particular titles. Rejecting a *fixed* hierarchy does not imply rejecting discipline, monitoring, evaluation, and accountable leadership. Moreover, even as in capitalist companies, the ultimate sanction of dismissal will still exist, but with crucial differences. Beyond the democratic decision making process, at Northstart the threat of dismissal will not endanger the employee's survival. Other employment opportunities will be offered, and basic consumption needs are in any event, guaranteed. Nor would unemployment have any affect on the consumption opportunities of one's children or spouse. Moreover, dismissal would have to be ratified by the individual's council coworkers and then, if appealed, by higher councils as well. But to understand these finer points we need to describe actual workdays in production firms. So here is an average week at Northstart.

### Larry's Workweek

On Wednesday Larry sorts mail for a few hours. He does this one morning every tenth week. On Wednesday next week, for two hours he will help with general cleanup. The following Wednesday Larry will work the front desk. Next month Larry has a different rotation, but he always has rote tasks assigned on Wednesday morning.

Of course, should Larry want to trade responsibilities for a certain Wednesday, to attend his child's school play or tennis tournament, for example, this would be fine. Larry's rote work is evaluated by other Northstart members responsible for intervening if unscheduled task switching interrupts orderly functions.

The council for producing drama books has six work teams and Larry's does production on Wednesday, Thursday, and Friday afternoons. Although many employees prefer working on only one production project at a time, Larry happens to like doing a variety of different tasks simultaneously, so he's currently working on one drama as typesetter, one as designer, and a third as proofreader. The design and proofing are done in teams of three, and Larry is team leader for the former.

On alternate Monday afternoons, Larry's editorial council meets first in teams for an hour and then as a whole for two more hours to address concerns about possible new titles, complaints, and suggestions. Each week Larry also reads his share of submissions. Each title that Larry reads is also read by another member of the team and, after they give a summary report, if they both agree to reject, the submission is returned to its author unless some other member wishes to hold on to the title. If they both want others to read it, the book is held. If they disagree, a team vote decides whether to reject the title or approve it for more serious evaluation.

Each week, Larry also works on his allotment of manuscripts that have passed initial evaluation. Which manuscripts he reads depends partly on his preferences and partly on how much time he and other members have for new assignments. Ultimately, books are accepted or rejected after everyone is ready to vote. Majority rules with serious attention to strong feelings of minorities.

Once accepted, each title goes to a particular team member, who becomes its editor. Larry has responsibility for editorial work on three titles.

On the Mondays that Larry doesn't have editorial meetings he sometimes attends the biweekly Northstart policy meeting as a representative of his editorial/production council. Each of the three editorial/production councils, the four business area councils, and any major policy work teams that happen to be functioning at the moment send representatives. Representatives serve for six meetings each year, with rotation staggered so that each council always has a representative who has attended at least the four previous meetings. At these sessions, personnel representatives report on problems, sometimes asking for help with interpersonal conflicts, and the general progress of the press's efforts is discussed and evaluated. On the Tuesday following policy meetings, editorial and business councils meet for an hour to hear reports. Special teams discuss reports whenever they can arrange time.

The rest of Larry's work is concerned with promotion, where he is currently helping produce a new catalog, working with potential authors, and soliciting new plays. He schedules this into his work week, along with cleaning his own office, updating his own files, and impromptu rote tasks shared with others.

Details of Northstart's arrangement seem sensible to Larry and his workmates but may not appeal to other publishing houses. Different workplaces could adopt longer or shorter timelines and adapt other practices as well. While basic principles must be respected, how they are implemented changes from workplace to workplace due to different conditions and from time to time in each workplace as preferences change.

To continue, Larry is gay and meets every eighth Thursday with other gay workers to discuss the character of editorial and business decisions and the changing patterns of daily work in light of the particular needs, tastes, and values of gay employees. Suggestions are often brought back to work teams and councils and sometimes to the whole Northstart collective. If these caucuses feel threatened by proposals otherwise supported by majorities of workers at Northstart, they may bring their complaints to outside councils.

There are countless possibilities for improved efficiency and a release of productive capability for useful purposes, in the U.S. economy. For instance, there are 49,000 hotels and lodging places employing 1.3 million people. Considering vacancy rates ranging from 5 percent to over 80 percent depending on the season and locale, how many of these could be put to other uses? Consider similar calculations for redundancy of other services and establishments? Then consider the gains that might be had by eliminating institutions that are necessary in a capitalist economy but useless in a participatory one, such as brokerage houses, insurance companies, banks, the IRS, FBI, and CIA.

### Northstart Efficiency

The reader may wonder:

1. Won't Northstart workers be frustrated because work is too fragmented? Is this a road to enrichment or psychosis?

2. Won't it take endless hours to train people for so many jobs? Is this excellence or institutionalized chaos?

3. Won't people ignore the authority of "leaders" on team A, when these same "leaders" are subordinate on team B?

*"We say only that pain can be diminished and pleasure enhanced by overcoming unnecessarily authoritarian, alienating, unfair, and uninformed facets of work life—not that all work can be transformed into distilled ecstasy."*

*"Under participatory economics, since all do rote work, all will want to minimize it. Since everyone does creative work, everyone will want to increase the amount to go around and no one will lose their livelihood if automation eliminates rote tasks workers disliked in the first place."*

4. Will one's co-workers provide enough motivation and oversight to prevent shoddy, dilatory work?

In answer to question 1—won't fragmentation frustrate North-start workers?—first, having many responsibilities makes work life richer and more diverse and is therefore positive, not negative. Of course, tasks and schedules could be fragmented to the point of distraction, but if a group decides it has "gone overboard," it has only to make the required correction.

Changing from capitalist to participatory economics would mean that instead of most people doing rote work all the time—and being bored most of the time—everyone will spend at least some of their work day doing interesting work. Moreover, because boring tasks will be distributed equitably, these too will be more bearable, though certainly not joyful. We do not claim that digging ditches, pushing buttons, or dangerous work will become joyful merely because one does it in a good society, at one's own pace, and in teams with friends, much less because one basks in the glow of some great leader or is sustained by the memory of some long-passed revolutionary upheaval. We say only that pain can be diminished and pleasure enhanced by overcoming unnecessarily authoritarian, alienating, unfair, and uninformed facets of work life—not that all work can be transformed into distilled ecstasy.

Moreover, there will be every reason to automate or eliminate rote work whenever doing so will enhance productivity or diminish the human burdens of work. Under capitalism automation is a crucial area of conflict between labor and capital—capitalists seek to enhance profits by automating some people's livelihood out of existence while workers try to defend their jobs to avoid becoming obsolete and unemployed. Under participatory economics, since *all* do rote work, *all* will want to minimize it. Since *everyone* does creative work, *everyone* will want to increase the amount to go around and no one will lose their livelihood if automation eliminates rote tasks workers disliked in the first place.

Question 1 really comes down to what happens to people who under capitalism have responsibilities which are almost entirely interesting and empowering. Yes, in participatory workplaces such work complexes will disappear because everyone will share rote work. Elementary justice dictates this, just as elementary justice dictates that consumption opportunities greatly in excess of average consumption must be eliminated. Those who have benefited from coordinator monopolization of desirable work will resist job balancing just as capitalists who monopolize wealth will resist income balancing. Both capitalists and coordinators advance arguments to justify their advantages but the truth is, in both cases, these arguments are fanciful, self-serving rationalizations. In fact, even those who now do no rote work need not be any more "fragmented" by having to do some cleaning, filing, and production than they are currently. For under systems in which they monopolize desirable work opportunities, these people are constantly distracted by having to always oversee others even as they regulate their own behavior in the presence of superiors. Anyway, anyone who knows anything about business in capitalism knows that upper-level workers spend much of the time they are not worrying about protocol day-dreaming, chatting on the phone, or designing and scrapping projects that will never be implemented. Beside being a waste of productive talent, this is not even a particularly enjoyable way to idle time away.

In answer to question 2—won't it take endless hours to train people for balanced job complexes?—at Northstart, training everyone to do editorial, business, *and* production work will admittedly take more time than training people to do just one of the three types of work. Likewise, developing skill in three areas will certainly take longer then developing skill in only one. But the mutually enforcing benefits of knowing more about each type of work, the enrichment that comes from having diverse responsibilities, and the increase in morale that accompanies understanding the whole publishing process will more than offset these additional training costs.

Or, if workers in a particular publishing house prefer the savings from reduced training over the benefits of greater diversity, then, provided equitable job complexes can be arranged in which each worker has fewer differently skilled responsibilities, workers can choose this option.

In answer to question 3—won't useful, needed lines of authority deteriorate if there are no fixed hierarchies?— respect for a team leader need not be undercut because she is in a nonleader role on other teams. At Northstart respect for leaders will depend on the logic of particular assignments and the need for tight coordination, oversight, or scheduling in those assignments. Far from diminishing the credibility of *legitimate* leadership, eliminating fixed hierarchies will undercut many impediments to efficient expression of leadership, for example, class hostilities.

In answer to question 4—will there be sufficient motivation?— the desire to do a good job worth doing, and, when necessary, peer pressure and the desire to keep one's job will more than adequately ensure that people work hard. Of course there will be disagreements and personality clashes. But surely these will be more manageable once demeaning hierarchy is eliminated. Intractible personality clashes will eventually be resolved by transfers. Arguments about who is doing how much work, how well, how hard, and with what degree of sympathy for coworkers, will be resolved by participants, or, when necessary, through council oversight. Sometimes "firing" will occur, but not at the whim of a "boss" or in such a way as to threaten one's income. In essence, the workday at Northstart is self-managed in the context of assessing the collective's well-being and its desires to publish desired books in an effective, efficient fashion. The only inflexible rules are those precluding methods that obstruct participation or deny equitable access of all workers to equal opportunities for fulfillment and influence.

We should note, however, that since the Northstart work complex has more creative and fewer distasteful qualities than the

We refuse to buy the right not to die of hunger by running the risk of dying of boredom.

—Student Slogan, Paris 1968

*"The only inflexible rules are those precluding methods that obstruct participation or deny equitable access of all workers to equal opportunities for fulfillment and influence."*

He, who before was the money owner, now strides in front as capitalist; the possessor of labor-power follows as his laborer. The one with an air of importance, smirking, intent on business; the other hesitant, like one who is bringing his own hide to market and has nothing to expect but—a hiding.
—Karl Marx
*Capital*

average workplace in the economy, Northstart workers have to put in some of their worktime elsewhere. Some Northstart employees work in community clean-up squads. Others do rote tasks at a neighboring plant that produces computer equipment. In any event, everyone does his or her share of outside work to balance the relative advantage of working at Northstart.

Would a sensible person rather work at a capitalist or participatory publishing house? Since we have not yet described allocation, we only partially understand how participatory economic decisions are made. But allocation-related issues aside, the quality of participatory work should be obviously superior.

1. The hassles of hierarchies disappear.

2. The pleasures of publishing for human well-being rather than capitalist profits are significant.

3. Opportunities for personal development and camaraderie with coworkers abound.

4. No one does solely debilitating, subordinate work.

Though work at Northstart isn't without conflict and drudgery, it is nonetheless a generally pleasurable and enriching means to personal development and integrity within a supportive community of coworkers.

# Airport Council Structure

Ignoring, for the sake of discussion, the probability of major changes in air transport owing to technological advances and ecological constraints, we next consider an airport.

Obviously an airport involves flying, air-traffic control, fueling, procuring and storing fuel, and repairing and maintaining aircraft, as well as keeping track of and ordering new equipment. In addition, there is providing service on the planes, procuring and preparing food for flights, handling baggage, making seating assignments, providing ground transportation, caring for the premises, and serving food and providing magazines, candy, and gum at terminals. Other necessary tasks include scheduling work assignments, preparing timetables for flights, and assessing demand.

## A Capitalist Airport

How should all this be organized? A capitalist airport (each of whose units are to make maximum profit) will fragment tasks into roles that give a minimum number of people authority. Pilots fly. Air-traffic controllers control traffic. Cooks cook. Baggage handlers handle baggage. Custodians clean. Food servers serve. Each job fosters different skills and imparts different rewards. Tremendous energy goes into coercing work from those at the bottom and competing for advancement at the top.

At a large capitalist airport, a huge number of individuals have marginal assignments that diminish solidarity with most of their coworkers and provide threadbare income and little fulfillment. A smaller number of pilots, administrators, and managers do interesting work but feel ambivalent about having to adapt themselves in elitist ways owing to the power they necessarily exert over their less exalted airport coworkers.

## A Participatory Airport

At Jesse Owens Airport—organized according to the principles of participatory economics—all workers participate intellectually, emotionally, and physically. This doesn't mean they all fly, cook, traffic-control, and organize schedules. As normal folks they have normal capacities, though these are well-developed because they have been schooled in a humane society. So, how do they achieve their goals? Of the many ways workers at Jesse Owens Airport could organize tasks into job complexes to insure a diversified and fulfilling work situation for all personnel, we summarize one.

First, an airport-wide council represents all workers at Jesse Owens airport. This global council in turn incorporates airplane task councils, ground task councils, and coordinating task councils. Each employee does either airplane or ground work and some coordinating work. There are also work-group councils for baggage handlers, restaurant workers, etc.

Airplane jobs include flying, navigating, and serving patrons. Ground jobs include procuring and storing fuel, maintaining and repairing airport vehicles and equipment, handling baggage, making seat assignments, providing food in the terminals, maintaining shops and airport grounds, air traffic control, and providing ground transport. Lastly, coordinating tasks include ordering supplies, scheduling flights, planning, and maintaining and overseeing operations and timetables.

Each Jesse Owens employee has a work complex that includes some coordinating *and* some plane or ground work. Assignments are in accord with the individual's tastes and skills and the general requirement that work complexes balance quality of work life. Not everyone is a pilot. Nor is everyone an air-traffic controller or personnel coordinator. However, more people do these types of work, for fewer hours, than in a capitalist airport. Those who pilot part of the week also serve patrons or handle baggage and do some coordinating work in a combination that gives them rewards and empowerment roughly comparable to people who don't pilot the plane but cook on it or fuel it.

On a particular flight someone will be in charge of services and someone else will be head pilot, and, if a team handles baggage, one member may be in charge. But a few individuals do not *always*

*"Tremendous energy goes into coercing work from those at the bottom and competing for advancement at the top."*

Accordingly, in proportion as work is broad or narrow, stimulating or monotonous, it develops or stunts one's abilities. Moreover, since individuals develop their personalities and consciousness through the way they relate to productive activity, work is a basis for the formation of consciousness along class lines.
—Sam Bowles and Herb Gintis, *Schooling In Capitalist America*

have authority, while others are *always* subordinate. The mythology that fixed hierarchies are the only efficient way to organize work disappears as job complexes balanced for participation and equity prove otherwise.

Obviously, it pays to diversify rote tasks. Training for these takes little time and benefits accruing from increased diversity and equity are substantial. For more complex work, like being a gourmet cook, a pilot, or an air-traffic controller, those trained would have to use their skills often enough to avoid the inefficiencies of investing heavily in training folks who do not put their training to sufficient use. However, even in these cases the notion that people should work exclusively at one task is an exaggeration.

Whereas at a capitalist airport an air-traffic controller would work a fifty- and sometimes a sixty-hour week and develop tension-related ailments, at Jesse Owens she would do air traffic work for only twenty hours and spend the rest of her time doing low tension tasks during which she could interact pleasantly with coworkers. While a flight attendant on a capitalist plane must always cater to passengers in a solicitous, menial way regardless of their behavior, at Jesse Owens he might have piloted an earlier flight, and then worked handling baggage and in the finance/planning office for the rest of the week. Moreover, when attending to the needs of passengers he would not be motivated by a desire to avoid being fired or to upstage fellow workers, but by a desire to provide a pleasant trip, good service, and quality work as a member of a team producing a worthy product. This would never require being servile. All work would be "humanized" as people's motives emphasize working for one's peers. Indeed, this typifies the change from a class-structured (and race- and gender-stratified) workplace in which motives develop in light of conflicts with one's coworkers and the desire to avoid getting screwed, to a self-managed workplace where one respects one's coworkers and enjoys the solidarity and pleasure of diverse work providing a socially useful product.

Some workers might have a work complex with especially rewarding and empowering tasks offset by turns at debilitating, boring tasks. Others might have more uniform complexes without work of either extreme. What wouldn't be possible is for workers to have only one extreme type of work, whether rote, aesthetic, responsible, or subordinate. If piloting were a desirable assignment and cleaning the insides of airplanes or toilets was not, we would often find that those who do one do some of the other as well. Is this a waste of talent and training? Could we get more hours of flying per hours of pilot training by having pilots only fly? Yes. But could we get a higher quality experience for airport workers and higher quality service for passengers by the more elite system of organization? No.

Jesse Owens airport would not lack means of supervision, coordination, and work evaluation. Personnel workers would evaluate and mediate. Team leaders would coordinate and supervise. Coun-

*"What wouldn't be possible is for workers to have only one extreme type of work, whether rote, aesthetic, responsible, or subordinate."*

cils would evaluate complaints, determine schedules, set job complexes, refine work loads, and collectively organize the global airport production plan. The point isn't that under participatory economics, all need for delegation of authority, evaluation, and coordination would disappear. That's ridiculous. The claim is only that such tasks, like all others, can be accomplished in ways that do not establish fixed hierarchies or otherwise allocate work inequitably. If baggage handling requires a team leader, fine, but it needn't be the same person every day. And, in any event, the team leader will handle bags like everyone else.

Airport workers will be well educated and capable of harmonious, socially rich interactions in a context where these are promoted and rewarded. We are not claiming everyone will want to learn everything, or be equally good at everything, or that all who perform a task will be equally good at it. We only claim that people can perform and enjoy a variety of tasks, and certainly many more than current arrangements permit.

## Printing— A Third World Example

Our two examples have both been in developed settings, whether capitalist or participatory. Now imagine visiting an island country that has combined public ownership of the means of production with central planning in an underdeveloped economy. How might a printing establishment there compare to how it was before the antiimperialist revolution? How might a transformation to participatory economics bring further changes?

Assume that more pressing investment priorities and capitalist boycotts have left printing technology unchanged from neocolonial days. The plant includes two out-of-date printing presses, one using cold type and the other geared for old-fashioned photo-typesetting; banks of equipment of diverse lineage for stripping negatives and preparing type; layout rooms; assorted equipment for preparing negatives; space for storing paper and materials; space for storing incoming and outgoing copy; loading docks, and a lunch counter. What kind of work was done before and after the anti-colonialist revolution? What kind might be done after a transformation to participatory economics?

*"We are not claiming everyone will want to learn everything, or be equally good at everything, or that all who perform a task will be equally good at it. We only claim that people can perform and enjoy a variety of tasks, and certainly many more than current arrangements permit."*

### Newsday Press—The Neocolonized Version

Before the revolution, Simon Bolivar Press was called Newsday Inc. and its product was the U.S. magazine *Newsday*. All its engineers were from the U.S., and while many of its managers were from the island, almost all were trained in the U.S. Newsday Inc. was 80 percent owned by capitalists in New York and 20 percent by local capitalists who spent much time in Miami and Las Vegas.

What to produce, for whom, by what methods, work pace, and remuneration was decided by the local owners in consultation with the majority owners in the States. As a result, Newsday Inc.'s product had little economic, intellectual, or entertainment value for the island's citizens. Darker-skinned workers and women did the worst jobs. Marginal attention went to quality of work life.

When fumes, pace, tension, noise, or overbearing management wore down one set of employees, they were fired and new islanders were hired to replace them. To provide carrots alongside the stick, the top jobs for islanders paid enough to support a middle class life, while bottom levels paid bare subsistence. Yet, as long as one could last, work at Newsday Inc. beat hell out of unemployment, begging, going back to one's family in a rural village, or starving. Profits were exported to New York or Miami, or spent to sustain the luxurious lifestyle of the indigenous elite.

*"So the U.S. government provided aid. The army and police were decked out in style, officers were trained in Louisiana, arms were provided from firms in Connecticut."*

Of course, to maintain the tranquility of Newsday Inc. and the island's largely U.S-owned casinos, plantations, and import businesses, more was required. Remaining funds, after outsiders took their share, were insufficient to support and maintain the island's all-important military, police apparatus, and public services sufficiently to keep the system afloat. Something had to be done.

So the U.S. government provided aid. The army and police were decked out in style, officers were trained in Louisiana, arms were provided from firms in Connecticut. Officers received relatively high salaries in addition to being allowed to go berserk every so often to "improve morale" and enforce fear. The "legitimate" bill for all this plus ample bribes and overcharges was paid with funds from Washington raised from U.S. taxpayers. Services of use to local owners and U.S. visitors were maintained. The rest went to hell in a handcart. As repression increased, so did aid, this correlation being the most tenacious in U.S. international affairs since more repression means a more exploitable work force and higher profits for U.S. companies, and therefore more reason to send aid to buy more goodies for lackeys and arms for police and to pay more gravediggers.

Ultimately some of the island's more courageous citizens raised the consciousness and sparked the hopes of enough citizens to sustain a popular struggle against imperialism and throw out local and absentee rulers. Since victory, however, times have been tough. A vindictive economic boycott has isolated the country and made rebuilding difficult. Progress has had to wait on the task of overcoming the imperialist legacy of deprivation, ignorance, crime, and degradation. Nonetheless, the revolutionary movement consolidated power and transformed island life.

### Simon Bolivar Press—The Anti-Imperialist Version

Imagine we visit our island and interview Mario, the manager of the nationalized Simon Bolivar Press. He shows us around, describes the plant, and answers questions. Mario proudly reports that the press no longer prints what North Americans dictate. Since the revolution and until very recently emphasis was on books for school children and a few magazines. Now, since more modern printing facilities installed in a distant province produce all the books, Simon Bolivar prints almost exclusively magazines, brochures, flyers, and posters. Equipment is run down since spare parts are hard to get and there is little foreign exchange to replace outmoded pre-revolutionary models from the U.S. But unlike pre-revolutionary times, today all the skilled printers and engineers are from the island. Our manager friend is justifiably proud of the fact that he and all managers and staff are products of a school system that teaches all citizens without prejudice and a health-care and food system that keeps the island's citizenry healthy and comfortable. "There is no more colonialism. There is no more prostitution, gambling, export of our wealth and our lifeblood. We are independent and, despite Western hostility, we are making our mark in the world," says Mario.

He then takes us on a tour of the plant. The walls have a few posters but are otherwise bare. Paint and many other supplies from the West are in short supply due to trade sanctions. Most typewriters are old fashioned. Typesetting equipment is 10 to 25 years out of date. Ironically, given the embargo, technicians apologize for this, asking questions about new technologies. The staff and workers show amazing creativity and tenacity in their ability to scrounge parts and master the innards of their outdated equipment, keeping it productive long after it would have been written off elsewhere.

Workers have regular breaks and everyone earns enough to get by reasonably well in light of the low cost of living and fine social services. Those who have worked longer or hold more responsible or technical positions earn more, but promotions are frequent, training is offered to anyone who wants it, and lines of authority are more flexible than in the past. We observe that women are mostly assigned to typing and typesetting, and are told that these particular women like this work, but that anyone who wishes to do more interesting tasks can take free courses and move up when job openings occur. We are introduced to the female manager of the magazine-preparation wing, a highly responsible position. We ask what she earns relative to Mario, who manages the plant, and hear that her salary is a bit higher because she does more skilled labor. Sensing our surprise, Mario quickly adds that he has the perk of a company car. He claims he doesn't want us to get the wrong impression. They have done wonders with income distribution, but all is not perfect yet. They are still developing.

Mario is black, but so are most of the men who work in the noisier parts of the factory. He accepts our implicit criticism, but tells us change takes time. We see rooms where plates are prepared and can't get out quickly enough—the fumes are overpowering. We ask whether workers in this room get more time off or whether the job is rotated, and no one even understands our question. We explain

The life under the capitalist system was a life condemned to death below the earth—and your children also; that's what they were good for. They were lucky if they made sixth grade; that was really special. Only the strongest could work. Those without good physiques could not… Look, I don't mean this in any way personally, but listen American. There used to be a barrio here they called barrio americano, where only Americans lived, the administrators, technicians, and so forth; and on the door of their social club was a sign, "Only for members." Now there is a social club for all of us. We are all members now. Everyone.

—A Cuban miner, 1969

*"We see rooms where plates are prepared and can't get out quickly enough—the fumes are overpowering. We ask whether workers in this room get more time off or whether the job is rotated, and no one even understands our question."*

The duty of every revolutionary is to make the revolution. It is known that the revolution will triumph in America and throughout the world, but it is not for revolutionaries to sit in the doorways of their houses waiting for the corpses of imperialism to pass by. The role of Job doesn't suit a revolutionary. Each year that the liberation of America is speeded up will mean the lives of millions of children saved, millions of intelligences saved for culture, an infinite quantity of pain spared the people.

—Fidel Castro
*Fidel Castro Speaks*

that working in this room, or in the noisy parts of the printing room, is much less desirable than working in quieter, cleaner sections, so we wonder if there is any compensation or sharing. "No," they say, amused, "that would be impossible. But workers can go to school and get promotions."

This pattern repeats frequently throughout the tour. Without even asking, we continually hear about technology and characteristics of finished products. Every description is careful and passionate and whenever we ask, we also get lively responses about wages, promotions, and schedules. However, inquiries about social relations, decision-making, and job definition baffle our hosts. When we persist, they answer honestly and without irritation, but also without interest. Our hosts clearly find this part of the discussion a waste of time. Why bother to spend time discussing a dimension of work organization that simply must be the way it is?

We hear how schools have absorbed much scarce investment resources and how the whole new generation is now well educated. Now resources can be allocated to other ends as well, including improving the plant to eliminate smelly, dangerous fumes. We have no doubt that Mario means it and hopes for it. But he doesn't understand the notion that as long as such a room exists, no one should have to work there more than anyone else. He fails to note that fans would make a difference, much less that the whole plant could be involved in decision making. When we press the point, he isn't hostile to these ideas, just dubious. We ask which members of the new generation—all of whom have a good education—are going to accept work in the smelly room while others escape it, and he admits there will have to be changes. We ask what kind of

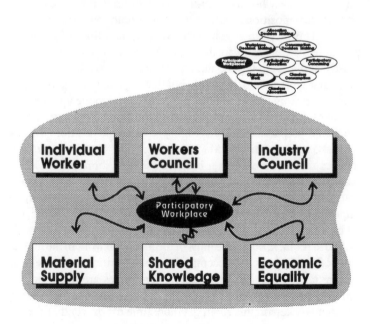

changes, and he says he doesn't know for sure but that already to get enough bus drivers—the buses are smelly and very crowded—new recruits have to be paid higher wages than many technicians and managers. When we ask whether he minds this, he says no, their work is uncomfortable and stressful and they deserve more. Mario is by no means a cynical defender of elite privileges. But idealism aside, he is at a loss for new ideas about job structure .

We get similar answers from everyone we talk with. The revolution has overcome imperialism, and this gives people pride and a feeling of accomplishment. The revolution has sharply reduced poverty, degradation, and ignorance, and greatly advanced the quality of life. But the revolution has not yet addressed issues of self-management or workers' solidarity. It is a coordinator economy with great elan and idealism among managers and technicians. But each day that these leaders deliver new orders and accumulate new advantages some of their idealism slips away. Workers enjoy vastly improved circumstances and have great hope for their children. But each day that they inhale fumes, obey orders, and get bored, some of their optimism dies. They are not prepared and may become steadily less prepared to govern their own workplaces and the economy as a whole. Democracy in opportunity *and* outcome, and in rewards *and* decision making, is absent. Even though the contrast to life for all but a tiny elite in other countries in the region is dramatic, it may prove insufficient in the eyes of most citizens if remaining problems are not addressed.

Let me say, with the risk of appearing ridiculous, that the true revolutionary is guided by strong feelings of love. It is impossible to think of an authentic revolutionary without this quality. This is perhaps one of the greatest dramas of a leader, [to] combine an impassioned spirit with a cold mind and make painful decisions without flinching one muscle... In these conditions one must have a large dose of humanity, a large dose of a sense of justice and truth, to avoid falling into dogmatic extremes, into cold scholasticism, into isolation from the masses... Above all, always be capable of feeling any injustice committed against anyone anywhere in the world. That is the most beautiful quality of a revolutionary.

—Che Guevara
Man and Socialism in Cuba

## *Simon Bolivar Press—The Participatory Version*

Assuming no change in level of economic development, what innovations would participatory economics bring to Simon Bolivar Press?

By now the answers should be fairly obvious. Just as throwing out capitalists and eliminating poverty, starvation, disease, and corruption were priorities of the anti-imperialist revolution, introducing workplace and consumer councils, egalitarian consumption, equitable job complexes, and collective self-management will be the goals of a participatory economic revolution.

Simon Bolivar Press would begin by rotating dangerous and debilitating tasks, reducing income inequalities, and increasing job training. But the goal of training would no longer be for trainees to escape undesirable jobs left behind for others to do, but to allow job complexes to be balanced with little or no loss of efficiency. Temporary disparities would persist only because of disparities in skills which would be steadily reduced. Plans for plant operations would be regularly distributed to the entire work force, whose proposals for alterations would be seriously considered before projects were undertaken. Workers at council meetings would propose projects and policies to be debated and voted on.

What do you suppose will satisfy the
soul except to walk free and
own no superior.
—Walt Whitman

Similarly, the plant's relationship to the island's planning board would change as plans from above were questioned, alternatives proposed, and finally, once enough experience and skill developed, Simon Bolivar along with other units would undertake decentralized participatory planning, first as an experiment running alongside traditional procedures, then as the main means of developing plans for the island.

The plant might still have a horribly smelly room for preparation of plates. But fans would improve things and all would work only short shifts in the smelly environment. Loading magazines onto trucks remains back-breaking work. Typesetting is still onerous. But employees who used to do one of these jobs all day long now spend somewhat less time on these tasks and more time on creative work or training. Mario spends more time not only in the plate preparation room, but on the presses and loading dock. He continues to do some managerial work, though without unilateral authority. The impetus for plant improvements, whether in the form of adjustments of job complexes, inexpensive innovations, or large-scale new technologies to eliminate burdensome and/or dangerous jobs, is greatly increased.

Since work at Simon Bolivar is less desirable than average, its workers work thirty-five hours there, putting in five hours in other plants or in their communities doing more enjoyable tasks like helping with day care and children's centers or community gardening. At more modern printing plants, job complexes are more pleasant than average. There, as a result, workers labor only thirty hours a week, putting in ten hours in agricultural and other hard labor in the vicinity. Job balancing committees had to make the initial calibrations, and now revise them on a continual basis taking note of disparities in job applications.

The result? In the transition from coordinator to participatory economics, incomes rise significantly for the lower-paid two-thirds of the Simon Bolivar work force. Quality of work life increases dramatically for those who previously did the lowliest tasks and considerably for most others. The quality of life drops materially but not psychologically for a relative few. Quality of product improves along with morale. Moreover, workers return home daily with more energy and more inclination to exert themselves in political and social life further improving work conditions, for example. Home life, community life, and political participation are thereby greatly enhanced.

A plant tour conducted a few years after participatory transformations would be punctuated primarily by descriptions of social relations and job complexes. We hear details of self-management. Workers speak of the change in morale and participation attendant on innovations. Product and technology are described with pride as well, but the emphasis is on why they were chosen, this having become the province of the workers rather than a distant planning elite.

From a display of the benefits of independence from imperialism, the island becomes a showcase for liberation from technocratic hierarchy. Organizing democratic workers' councils, balanced job complexes, and participatory planning was certainly difficult but not impossible in the absence of high technology. The point is that participatory organization can work wonders not only in work places with access to high tech methods, but also in plants with an excess of manual, dangerous, and debilitating labor, like those that still prevail in many parts of the U.S. and in most of the third world. To be sure, however, coordinators are likely to resist such changes that would undermine their privileges in the economy and in society as a whole.

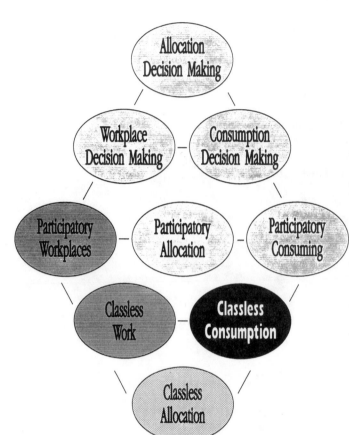

# Egalitarian Consumption

*What a sad and tragic mistake! To give full scope to socialism entails rebuilding from top to bottom a society dominated by the narrow individualism of the shopkeeper. It is not as has sometimes been said by those indulging in metaphysical woolliness just a question of giving the worker "the total product of his labor"; it is a question of completely reshaping the relationships...in the factory, in the village, in the store, in production, and in distribution of supplies. All relations between individuals and great centers of population have to be made all over again, from the very day, from the very moment one alters the existing commercial organization.*

*—Peter Kropotkin*

If production is at the foundation of every economy, consumption is the living room. How consumption is organized therefore affects the quality of life just as work organization does. Under capitalism when we buy, there is every incentive to think only of ourselves while ignoring the environment, our neighbors, and especially the workers who produce what we enjoy. In fact, in capitalism it is nonsensical to consider others.

Eating a salad, we do not assess the plight of migrant pickers. Driving a car, we do not calculate the increased probability of cancer for children playing on the sidewalks we pass. Even as we whimsically over consume what might help others survive, we ignore the human implications of our own gluttony. We know relatively little about others. We feel relatively little for others. We do relatively little to help others. Whatever our inclinations, markets provide means for us to consider only our own welfare. Regardless of our wishes, our scramble for goods impedes solidarity.

Yet even within the raging individualism of our capitalist economy we can imagine a particularly close-knit family that makes collective decisions. Such a family, in contrast to the usual patriarchal situation, might together allocate funds for family purchases and decide together how much each member can spend out of what's left over. And while individual purchases by the family's members may be primarily private, this may not be entirely so.

For example, given this family's special solidarity, perhaps all its members understand that every consumption decision has implications extending beyond the individual doing the consuming. Consider a son buying a set of drums or father purchasing a box of cigars. Since the byproducts of those purchases, noise and smoke, will affect everyone, the purchases are not really private. More interesting, a family member's consumption may affect his or her personality and then, by way of that, everyone in his or her social orbit. Consider the result if father spends his allowance on liquor, or if a daughter spends hers playing computer armageddon. Since the whole family will suffer, the family may justifiably intervene to maintain a subtle balance between privacy, freedom, and the need to promote an acceptable environment for everyone.

But these unusual family members we've dreamed up are able to weigh one another's circumstances only because they communicate considerable information to one another. Certainly few would suggest that such tight bonds could (or should) characterize relations between *all* citizens. After all, families actually live together. Yet if participatory economics could emulate our unusual small family's interpersonal concern for one another's well-being while simultaneously protecting each person's right to self-management and privacy, it would certainly help overcome the debilitating competition familiar to normal capitalist consumption patterns.

HUMONGO
MOBILE
2 MPG
2,000 HP

ECO-CAR
200 MPG
10 HP

To enjoy the things we ought, and to hate the things we ought has the greatest bearing on excellence of character.

—Aristotle
*The Basic Works of Aristotle*

## Consumption Norms

Some personal consumption decisions affect primarily one individual consumer and the workers who produce what he or she consumes. Other personal consumption decisions affect a broader spectrum of economic actors. The concept of an "externality," wherein an economic act affects people beyond those immediately involved is applicable in these instances and, in fact, all goods have varying degrees of external impact.

It follows that if every consumer is to have a say roughly proportional to the effects they feel, and if economic decisions are to promote variety and solidarity, we need a means for actors to interact with one another before decisions are reached. Moreover, for work to be socially beneficial as well as equitable, workers and consumers will have to interact as a critical part of planning their related economic activities. Though the means for consumers to interact with workers and with consumers in other councils depends on the allocation system still to be discussed, we can here address at least a means for consumers *within* particular councils to consider consumption requests.

Sell a country! Why not sell the air, the clouds, and the great sea as well as the earth?

—Tecumseh
*Speech to Governor Harrison*

## Consumption Councils

Participatory consumption will be organized into a system of increasingly larger consumers' councils and federations. Inside each council consumers make decisions collectively, sensitive to the right of individuals not to be bullied by majorities and to the importance of promoting variety. Clear communication between councils allows collective oversight without domination or infringement on privacy. Each individual determines what she or he wants in light of the well-being of the workers who produce what one hopes to consume.

In neighborhood consumers' councils members discuss the implications of consumption proposals for workers and formulate their requests accordingly. For now, we assume that allocation procedures help neighborhood councils know what allowance is available for improvements in the neighborhood and for private individuals' purchases. Three principles guide consumption decision making:

1. Decisions about collective consumption will be reached *collectively* and judged by all affected councils.

2. Decisions about budget allocations to each council member will depend on past histories, work experiences, and needs, subject to *collective oversight* to ensure equity and to allow experimentation.

3. Decisions about what individuals wish to consume will be subject to *collective criticism* by fellow council members, though with specific guarantees for preserving individual freedoms and privacy.

In our model, each neighborhood council is part of a larger ward, county, region, state, and national federation of councils. Larger units reach collective consumption decisions first since their choices often have implications for what lower unit and individual needs might be. For example, the decision for a county to establish a fully equipped athletic facility would naturally affect whether a neighborhood would want its own small athletic facility and whether individuals would want athletic equipment of their own.

Thus, by allowing groups to first decide collective consumption, the system ensures that "public goods" will be "purchased" with proportionate input from everyone affected before private decisions are made. Private decisions, in turn, will be made in light of collective choices.

## Participatory Policies

When people assess their wants and request products, what norms apply? What rules protect personal rights? Since money in its usual sense isn't used, a point we will address in more detail in

---

...the moment a man gets money so many men are trying to get it away from him that in a little while he regards the whole human race as his enemy and he generally thinks that they could be rich too if they only attend to business as he has. Understand, I am not blaming these people... We must remember that these rich men are naturally produced. Do not blame them. Blame the system.
—Robert Ingersoll
*A Lay Sermon*

*"...by allowing groups to first decide collective consumption, the system ensures that "public goods" will be "purchased" with proportionate input from everyone affected before private decisions are made."*

coming chapers, what assures equity? How are the well-being of the collective and each individual balanced?

If you think about how you would want others to relate to your consumption and how you would want to be able to relate to theirs, "natural norms" readily emerge. If you were seeking more than average, you would think it fair for others to ask why you should be allowed to have more than they. Similarly, you would want the right to make such inquiries of anyone who was requesting more than average.

We can imagine many explanations that would cause us to accept someone else's above-average request. For example, someone might have unusual needs owing to illness or to the requirements of some short-term project she was undertaking. In that case she might offer to consume less later in order to consume more now; in effect borrowing from later rights. Or someone might have consumed less in the past, thereby justifying above-average consumption now.

If a person did request more than average, she might be questioned, and if her answers were unconvincing, she would be asked to moderate her request. Even if someone ordered an average allotment or less, questions might arise about why someone would want items that seemed personally unsafe, just as families might raise such questions now. But no individual would be required to provide answers to such inquiries, nor would such requests be deniable by consumption council partners on such grounds. Indeed, the process could be anonymous, with the details of proposals entered in private and assessed without names attached so that there would be no built-in carte-blanche, busybody mode or even an excessively normative method of thinking about consumption. All we are saying is that since each person's consumption affects the whole community, people operating in solidarity with one another may wish to express their feelings about unusual, socially intrusive or dangerous requests. If a consumption request indicates that I have an alcoholic neighbor, while anonymity will prevent me from knowing who, I can still urge restraint and counseling to the anonymous individual.

The sanctity of each person's choice is thus preserved by their privacy and their right to consume anything that won't endanger others up to their budgetary allotment, and also by the right to consume, if preferred, entirely as an individual by being a one-person council, though such behavior would entail losing many collective conveniences. On the other hand, the collective's right to adjudicate excessive requests and to argue against antisocial or otherwise deleterious consumption is also preserved. We can now describe a first pair of norms for consumption behavior.

1. To guarantee equity there must be a measure of average per capita consumption for individuals, neighborhoods, regions, and states, and there must be a way to ensure that individuals, neighborhoods, regions, and states don't

Good sense is of all things in the world most equally distributed, for everybody thinks he is so well supplied with it, that even those most difficult to please in all other matters never desire more of it than they already possess.
—Rene Descartes
*The Discourse On Method*

*"All we are saying is that since each person's consumption affects the whole community, people operating in solidarity with one another may wish to express their feelings about unusual, socially intrusive or dangerous requests."*

I were better to be eaten to death with
rust than to be scoured to nothing with
perpetual motion.
—Shakespeare
*Henry IV*

consume above average amounts unless they receive permission from others to do so. Requests for goods and services that place an above average burden on society's productive potentials may be rejected by consumer councils on equity grounds.

2. To guarantee the right to privacy and personal control of one's purchases, average- and below-average requests must not be subject to aggressive oversight and, should they want to suffer the losses involved in forsaking the benefits of collective consumption goods, individuals must be free to act as their own one-person consumption councils.

At first, this system may sound excessively time-consuming or intrusive. As we proceed, we will see how it will actually take less time and respect each actor more than capitalist consumption does. As for accounting, though it sounds like it would require a traditional market pricing and payment system, we will soon present alternative allocation procedures more consistent with participatory goals.

The second norm that would regulate participatory consumption involves a subtle balance between the needs of consumers and the needs of producers. Whenever consumers request more of a product than producers currently propose to produce, an evaluation must occur. Is the excess demand for a good simply the result of misallocating workers and resources? If so, workers and resources will be shifted from some industries to others. Or is the excess demand general? In which case a debate over the desirable level of consumption versus leisure trade-off must take place. Concretely, do we want to switch workers from relatively under-desired radishes to relatively over-desired peaches? Do I really want to work more so peach consumers can have their fill? Or do I really want to order so many peaches when peach workers are already overburdened and no additional workers can be easily transferred to the task?

We have already established that in a participatory economy each individual works at a roughly average job complex and requests a roughly average consumption bundle that may differ greatly in their particular contents. We are assuming, until we can demonstrate the point, that requests and "offerings" can be reconciled by our planning system in a way that maintains equity and collective self-management while promoting an efficient use of resources. Though we can build into the system that workers and consumers account for one another's needs, of course we must anticipate that often consumers will request more of certain goods than workers are prepared to produce. In such cases, our allocation dynamic must promote equitable solutions, but even before we describe how participatory allocation will efficiently and humanely equilibrate supply and demand, we can usefully make a few points about regulating consumption here.

First, within reason one should be able to increase one's consumption in a certain year not only by consuming less in the prior

*"One of our responsibilities is to contribute to society and fulfill our social capacities by working to our abilities. A derivative right is to enjoy the fruits of generalized economic labor by consuming our fair share."*

year, or saving, but also by pledging to consume less in a forthcoming year, or borrowing. Similarly, one should be able to work harder or longer to "earn" additional purchasing power to be able to "afford" a special trip or a new home computer. How is this to occur?

As the reader will have noticed by now, under participatory economics we do not "earn" an income that gives us a right to then spend, in the traditional sense. Instead, one of our responsibilities is to contribute to society and fulfill our social capacities by working to our abilities. A derivative right is to enjoy the fruits of generalized economic labor by consuming our fair share.

In participatory economies not everyone must choose to exert exactly equal efforts in production in exchange for exactly equal consumption rights. The overall principle is that consumption should be correlated to effort or personal sacrifice for the social good. But participatory economies should permit individuals to work harder for extra consumption or less hard for less consumption if they wish, provided that the results are not socially destructive.

In our discussion of the workplace we explained that everyone would work at a socially average job complex. When an individual has a job complex in a particular workplace with characteristics that are less desirable than average, he or she spends some of the work day doing more desirable work elsewhere. Likewise, those with job complexes at a workplace whose qualities are of above average

We already foresee a state of society where the liberty of the individual will be limited by no laws, no bonds—by nothing else but his own social habits, and the necessity which everyone feels, of finding cooperation, support, and sympathy among his [or her] neighbors.
—Kropotkin
*Revolutionary Pamphlets*

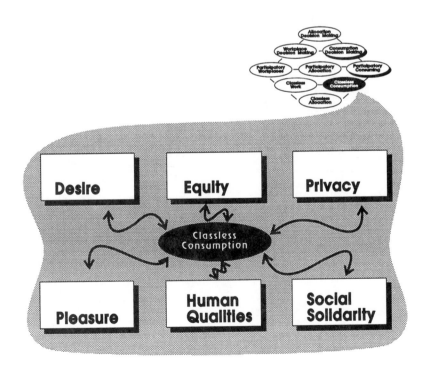

Dehumanization, which marks not only those whose humanity has been stolen, but also (though in a different way) those who have stolen it, is a distortion of the vocation of becoming more fully human... This, then, is the great humanistic and historical task of the oppressed: to liberate themselves and their oppressors as well.

—Paulo Freire
*Pedagogy of the Oppressed*

desirability spend time doing rote tasks elsewhere so people's total work has roughly the same qualitative impact. This being true, the number of hours a person works can serve as a rough measure of one's contribution in the sense of inconvenience or personal sacrifice underwent for other's benefit. If one wanted to "over-work" to later "over-consume," one would only need to work extra average hours. Equity and solidarity would be preserved.

All able-bodied adults are expected to work the social average number of hours at a socially average job complex. This total emerges as a function of people's overall collective desire for goods, services, and investments for future growth, as compared with their desire for free time. Everyone who does so is entitled to a bundle of goods (or savings) whose value equals the societal average. Those who want to ask for more may do so. They may borrow on future consumption, collect on past savings, cash in on extra work performed, or ask for others' permission to consume above average for special reasons. Modest consumption requests are immune to veto by fellow consumers, thus ensuring individual freedom and the right to experiment, though when it appears harmful any request *may* be discussed. Also, those who want to work less may do so, up to a point and if they can find a workplace that will accommodate them, by also agreeing to consume less.

Collective decisions are made before individual requests and decided by majority vote though strong minorities are given every opportunity not only to make their case, but also to devise compromise collective consumption requests acceptable to all. Every effort is made to ensure that everyone not only has a say, but that everyone influences final collective decisions. In the next chapter, specific examples clarify consumption norms further.

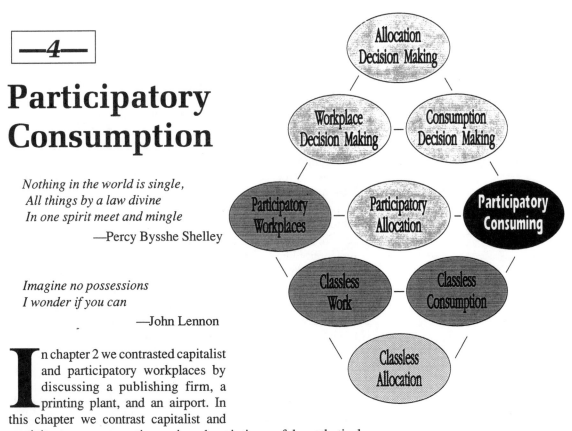

# —4—

# Participatory Consumption

*Nothing in the world is single,*
*All things by a law divine*
*In one spirit meet and mingle*
　　　　　　—Percy Bysshe Shelley

*Imagine no possessions*
*I wonder if you can*
　　　　　　　—John Lennon

In chapter 2 we contrasted capitalist and participatory workplaces by discussing a publishing firm, a printing plant, and an airport. In this chapter we contrast capitalist and participatory consumption using descriptions of hypothetical people, a co-housing community, and counties to clarify alternatives. We describe a few possible ways of organizing activity while recognizing that many other choices would be equally compatible with participatory norms.

## Collective Consumption

### *The Capitalist Case*

How are the million citizens of a capitalist county organized so that their different desires emerge as demands for "public" goods? Who decides? Who pays?

We need to consider purchases of roads, schools, hospitals, parks, fire equipment, and social services. Yet this does not exhaust the list of "things" consumed collectively by members of the county we'll call Jefferson Park.

For example, there is the look of the county, largely determined by its architecture. And there is the county's ecological health, determined by pollution standards and availability of ecologically sound goods. Thus not only those goods usually deemed "public," compose the county's "collective consumption."

His name was George F. Babbitt,
and...he was nimble in the calling of
selling houses for more than people
could afford to pay.
—Sinclair Lewis
*Babbitt*

In capitalist Jefferson Park, the county government decides on the mix of public goods and what taxes will be levied to pay for them. But in capitalist Jefferson Park the government inevitably caters to lobbies that wield power in proportion to their wealth. Traffic lights are erected and streets repaved in upper- and middle-class areas. Toxic wastes are dumped in the ghetto. County government also determines the location of public and private buildings by setting zoning ordinances in response to pressure, wealth being more important than numbers of voters.

Consider hospitals. How many are in Jefferson Park county? How are they designed? What ailments do they treat? The number of private hospitals depends on whether they attract investors, which in turn depends on the county government's efforts to provide services. The number of public hospitals will depend on the county budget, which is in turn affected by the tax base held hostage by business. In a system where those who pay the piper call the tune, design of any hospital and disposition of its resources will naturally reflect the tastes of its financers. If a hospital's clientele is wealthy, providing attractive rooms, fine care, and a maximum of amenities justifies high prices and the hospital is private. If the hospital's clientele is poor, much of its revenue must come from the county budget and budget crises will necessitate reducing costs and increasing "throughput" per day. Amenities won't translate into profits. The disposition of resources is geared to speed and thrift, not comfort or care.

The influence of money over county policy gives rise to a "sensible" popular passivity in Jefferson Park. With less time free from the daily struggle for survival, and county officials already beholden to wealthy donors, county politics for the majority reduces to ignorance and passivity regarding important decisions interrupted by occasional outbursts of rage at corruption, incompetence, or a tax burden grossly out of proportion to benefits received. The result is that most of the populace have little input into deciding whether a hospital should be constructed, what its design should be, and whom it should serve. The same holds for construction and repair of roads, fire stations, airports, the location of factories, the location and quality of schools, libraries, recreation centers, and health clinics, and the mixture and incidence of taxes to pay for them. The people most affected rarely influence results. Most Jefferson Park "consumers" never even know what issues are at stake.

In every cry of every man,
In every infant's cry of fear,
In every voice, in every ban,
The mind-forged manacles I hear.
—William Blake,
*London*

What alternatives are there? What could we do other than leave decisions to government bureaucrats?

Conservatives insist that the solution lies in taking decisions out of the hands of "government"—whose decisions are often corrupt and—according to Milton Friedman—biased and "necessarily" coercive, and leaving them to the market where "all choices are voluntary and freedom is preserved." But this is nonsensical. Decisions about parks, roads, schools, and fire protection are decisions that affect a large number of people. Even mainstream economists have long recognized there is nothing efficient, much less democratic, about leaving such decisions to the market place. These decisions should be collectively made. The trick is how to do so in a way that guarantees everyone an equal and effective opportunity to participate without wasting their valuable time.

### The Participatory Case

In participatory Martin Luther King County (MLK), all citizens belong to their neighborhood council, their ward council, and the MLK council. With this structure, not all ward or county council members need to attend all ward or county council meetings. Sometimes, for really important issues, decisions are made by a referendum of all members. Other times, only representatives sent by neighborhood councils to ward councils or ward councils to county councils vote. Meetings are always open and for important issues they are televised before referenda. In addition, one county workplace is the Collective Consumption Facilitation Board (CCFB), which is empowered to facilitate decision making regarding county collective consumption. The CCFB is governed by the same participatory rules as any other workplace. Each neighborhood and ward council has its own smaller CCFB to facilitate their collective consumption decisions, and the same holds for cities, states, and regions.

So there is the "level" of each individual, the "level" of the neighborhood, the "level" of the ward, and the "level" of the county. To fully understand collective consumption requires relating it to the planning of all economic decisions which we discuss later. Here, however, we can describe relevant local institutions and the logic of some of their procedures.

MLK county determines short- and long-term collective consumption priorities and plans. It chooses between projects like new athletic complexes, cultural centers, hospitals, schools, bus systems, or no new construction at all.

The county council makes decisions by referendum of the whole council on a variety of proposed project menus. Competing collective consumption alternatives arise out of communications between the CCFB and county council representatives from neighborhood councils. The CCFB has data about prior years' plans as well as projects that were not approved last year. A first set of options includes a continuation of plans in progress, a listing of other plans previously desired but delayed, and a list of proposals for possible new collective consumption projects received by the CCFB from neighborhood councils, individuals, and workplaces during the year.

Planning procedures (discussed in the next two chapters) then refine these many possibilities into more precise options so that choices can be made by a county referendum. Although additional participation by citizens requires more of their time go to managing collective consumption, they spend less time influencing these

I think that I shall never see
A billboard lovely as a tree,
Indeed, unless the billboards fall
I'll never see a tree at all.
—Ogden Nash
*Song of the Open Road*

collective participatory plans than they previously spent compensating for the lack of social services induced by profit-motivated market decisions.

Once the county's collective consumption decisions are determined, ward and neighborhood councils consider issues such as improving collective day care facilities, scheduling food delivery, reseeding parks, changing pool schedules, building a new movie complex, and enlarging the local library. Neighborhood CCFBs facilitate such decisions by listing options and enumerating their likely effects. Instead of the whole county participating, only members of the affected ward or neighborhood cast "ballots," though ultimately each neighborhood's plan is summed into the plan for the whole county, and then summed into the plan for the whole society.

The difference between capitalist Jefferson Park County and participatory Martin Luther King County should be clear. In the capitalist case, collective consumption succumbs to the will of government bureaucracy and powerful private interests. Definition of options and their refinement into final choices rests with "professionals" subject to pressure by private lobbies. Most citizens are estranged from decisions, which accommodate only the wills of powerful elites motivated by a desire to maximize only their own profits and status.

In Martin Luther King County, individuals, neighborhoods, and interest groups submit ideas for collective consumption projects. Workers serving on the CCFB refine these options into coherent possibilities whose effects can be compared. Their workplaces are structured so that CCFB workers have no vested interests to advance, and in any event final collective consumption is debated by everyone who wishes to participate and final decisions are made by democratic votes sensitive to the different effects decisions may have on different constituencies.

> Why should workers agree to be slaves in a basically authoritarian structure? They should have control over it themselves. Why shouldn't communities have a dominant voice in running the institutions that affect their lives?
> —Noam Chomsky
> *Language and Politics*

*"In Martin Luther King County, individuals, neighborhoods, and interest groups submit ideas for collective consumption projects."*

# Individual Consumption

## *The Capitalist Case*

In capitalism, shopping is the quintissential economic activity. Live to shop; shop 'til you drop. But in capitalism when we consume we know little about what others must do to produce what we consume. Even if we wanted to we have limited ability to temper our requests out of concern for producers. We can only respect the limits of what is available, of our personal budget, and of our own desires.

But what determines availability? The aims and motives of owners, a fact which significantly restricts consumer options. And what tells us what the market offers? Packaging, advertising, and word of mouth, none of which is entirely trustworthy. And what determines our budget? Wages, income, and other forms of private grossly unequal wealth. And what additional pressures influence us to buy more of this or that? The norms of gender, class, and culturally circumscribed behavior that we must "live up to," the requirements of work, the pressures of seeking status through consumption, and, in the absence of viable social alternatives, the need to find almost all enjoyment from private commodities.

The absurdity of consumption under capitalism is difficult for us "insiders" to recognize. In *The Dispossessed,* (Avon, 1974), science-fiction writer, Ursula LeGuin, has a character named Shevek from a planet devoid of consumerism visit a capitalist shopping mall. His reaction is as follows: "Saemtenevia Prospect was two miles long, and it was a solid mass of things to buy, things for sale. Coats, dresses, gowns, robes, trousers, breeches, shirts, umbrellas, clothes to wear while sleeping, while swimming, while playing games, while at an afternoon party, while at an evening party, while at a party in the country, while traveling, while at the theater, while riding horses, gardening, receiving guests, boating, dining, hunting—all different, all in hundreds of different cuts, styles, colors, textures, materials. Perfumes, clocks, lamps, statues, cosmetics, candles, pictures, cameras, hassocks, jewels, carpets, toothpicks, calendars, a baby's teething rattle of platinum with a handle of rock crystal, an electrical machine to sharpen pencils, a wristwatch with diamond numerals, figurines and souvenirs and kickshaws and mementos and gewgaws and bric-a-brac, everything

Fixed like a plant on his peculiar spot,
To draw nutrition, propagate, and rot.
—Alexander Pope
*An Essay on Man*

A touch of dishonesty is part of the very existence of private merchandising. When a peasant buys a horse, he runs it down in every possible way. If he sells the same horse a year later, it will have become younger, better, and stronger... One's own commodity will always be the best—the other person's the worst. Deprecation of one's competitors—a deprecation that is usually devoid of all honesty—is an essential tool of one's business.
—Wilhelm Reich
*The Mass Psychology of Fascism*

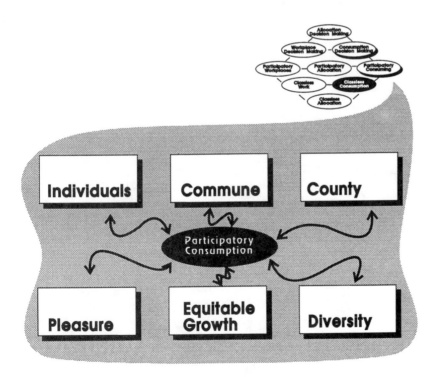

Ring out old shapes of foul disease,
Ring out the narrowing lust for gold;
Ring out the thousand wars of old,
Ring in the thousand years of peace.
—Alfred North Tennyson
*Collected Works*

either useless to begin with or ornamented so as to disguise its use; acres of luxuries, acres of excrement. After one block Shevek had felt utterly exhausted. He could not look any more. He wanted to hide his eyes. But to Shevek the strangest thing about the nightmare street was that none of the millions of things for sale were made there. They were only sold there. Where were the workmen, the miners, the weavers, the chemists, the carvers, the dyers, the designers, the machinists, where were the hands, the people who made? Out of sight, somewhere else. Behind walls. All the people in all the shops were either buyers or sellers. They had no relation to the things but that of possessions. How was he to know what a goods' production entailed? How could they expect him to decide if he wanted something? The whole experience was totally bewildering. Were his hosts in this strange world, the 'shoppers' of A-Io, really capable of such daily acts of social irresponsibility?"

### The Participatory Case

Some Martin Luther King county citizens will live alone and others in traditional families. Some will live with a few friends and others will live in "co-housing communities" where many dwellings band together as a larger whole to collectively share various resources, responsibilities, etc. All these different kinds of living units will be members of their neighborhood consumption council.

As one of the more collective forms of living group people might choose, what might a co-housing community be like? Emma

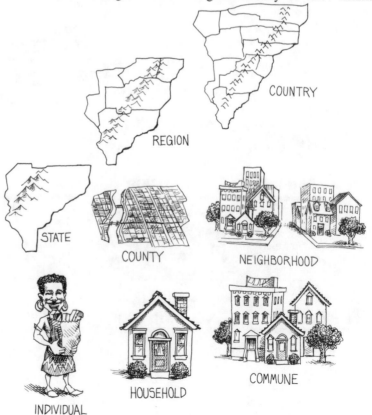

Goldman community (EG) has sixty-seven members, of whom thirty-five range from a few months to seventeen-years-old. Of the thirty-two "adults," twenty-four are "coupled" and eight "uncoupled." Eight of the children have biological parents living as a couple in the complex. Another twelve have both biological parents living in the complex but not "coupled." Nine of the remaining fifteen children have one biological parent living with them and the other either deceased or living elsewhere. Four of the children have a biological parent or parents who live elsewhere, but none in the complex.

EG community has households of various types. A quarter of the couples are gay and many people live in extended families. The complex has a children's quarter and an adult-quarter where children and adults can enjoy privacy from one another. The community's households all have pleasant individual living quarters and adequate kitchen facilities, but EG also has a dining hall, collective sports equipment, a large library and entertainment center, a collective laundry room, and a computer center.

The EG community meets regularly to adopt and update consumption plans, coordinate schedules for day care, shopping, and other tasks that exploit economies of scale. Clearly, the advantages of the co-housing community lie in this collectivizing feature—the sharing of tasks and responsibilities, the ready availability of assistance, baby sitters, friends, and project partners, and the advantage of not wasting personal consumption allowances on goods that can be enjoyed more cheaply, efficiently, and ecologically when shared collectively, such as laundry facilities, athletic resources, and high-quality hobby, computer, movie, or musical equipment.

So what is the situation of the individual consumer? First, he or she considers individual consumption in light of already determined collective plans for the county, neighborhood, and co-housing community, since these collective decisions may greatly affect needs for private consumption. Of course, carefully planned collective consumption does not relegate private consumption to the ashcan of history. There is plenty left to decide personally, and we must ask how this differs from consumption under capitalism.

Lydia belongs to EG community. She likes it because its membership, (which changes as some people leave and others are accepted by vote of the whole complex) is in tune with her own tastes. As with most communities, there is no smoking. People of diverse ages, sexual preferences, and cultural backgrounds are included. Most of the members of EG are into theatre, film, music, or writing. Their collective consumption decisions are made accordingly, so EG has less athletic equipment, science labs, and crafts rooms than other co-housing communities, but enjoys a small theatre, above-average sound systems, photo labs, and music rooms.

Lydia determines her personal consumption needs taking collective requests into account. She also considers the implications of her requests for workers with the aid of information generated by allocation procedures we have yet to discuss. Beyond being able to

I am an invisible man.... I am a man of substance, of flesh and bone, fiber and liquids—and I might even be said to possess a mind. I am invisible, understand, simply because people refuse to see me.

—Ralph Ellison
*The Invisible Man*

Buying and selling is essentially antisocial.

—Edward Bellamy
*Looking Backward*

consciously affect and take account of collective decisions, Lydia is also privy to the general character of her community mates' private consumption choices because she is allowed to question those that seem dangerous or otherwise antisocial at planning sessions whenever someone proposes to consume more than a fair allotment or whenever someone's (anonymous) consumption request is of such a character that Lydia (or anyone else) feels that it is potentially harmful either to the consumer or to the co-housing community as a whole. Of course, the same holds for Lydia's requests, which are put into the public hopper and seen by others, though without knowing which of all the requests they are examining is hers.

Because Lydia has to propose her consumption yearly doesn't mean she cannot change her requests when need arises. Participatory consumption welcomes regular updates of plans. Yet Lydia must get her food, furniture, clothes, and whatever else somewhere. Primarily, she will get it at local outlets in her neighborhood although she can also "make purchases" at outlets else-

PRODUCTION UNIT

PROPOSAL

CONSUMER

PROPOSAL

ITERATION BOARD

where should she want to. All this will become clearer as we present our description of allocation in the next chapter.

## To Consume or Be Consumed?

CAP: Why put obstacles in the way of people fulfilling themselves however they see fit? Your normative, busybody, socially responsible consuming sounds like torture.

PE: I'm just saying that we should consider our fellow citizens...

CAP: But you say people should judge one another's requests...

PE: I say consumption has private *and* public effects and that we ought to pay attention to both. I'm also saying that if some people have budgets thousands of times smaller than others, the fact that the poor can buy whatever they want within their budgets doesn't achieve much.

MARK: But once we eliminate capitalist ownership we eliminate gross inequality. And the market harmonizes private interests so they coincide with social interests. It is unnecessary as well as counter-productive to intrude on personal choice.

PE: The market doesn't deal efficiently with nonrenewable resources or account for how what happens in one plant affects others or even for the way the things I do affect you...

MARK: But what about privacy? Cap's right. Why should anyone know what I'm consuming?

PE: You aren't listening. Each person's list of consumption requests is accessible to others, but with no name attached. The total value you request is public and if you want to over-consume or borrow, that's public with people assessing the reasons you give. But why do you care if others comment if they feel your choices may be harmful? Your identity is secret. Your privacy is preserved. Only the requests, with no name attached, are public. And your neighbors cannot stop you from ordering what you want as long as your total request is commensurate with your work effort. Besides, aren't you impinging on my interests when you consume scotch and gin till you are nothing but a social parasite? What harm can come from others confronting what they believe is counter-productive behavior in hopes that doing so would help set the anonymous person associated with the behavior straight?

We're not talking about a state censor. There is no big brother, just harmless neighbors. In fact, there is no state at all, at least in the traditional sense of that word. People wouldn't want to waste their time assessing anonymous requests for food and books. But if some disturbed zealot does intrude, is it such a big deal? It will be annoying, but social pressure will certainly limit it. Occasional prying is a small price to pay for a system promoting solidarity.

I would like to believe that people have an instinct for freedom, that they really want to control their own affairs. They don't want to be pushed around, ordered, oppressed, etc., and they want a chance to do things that make sense, like constructive work in a way that they control, or maybe control together with others. I don't know any way to prove this. It's really a hope about what human beings are like—a hope that if social structures change sufficiently, those aspects of human nature will be realized.

—Noam Chomsky
*Language and Politics*

We want a socialist revolution with human nature as it is now, with human nature that cannot dispense with subordination, control, and managers.

—Lenin

I and the public know
What all schoolchildren learn,
That those to whom evil is done
Do evil in return.
—W. H. Auden
*September 1, 1939*

What-is it then makes people happy?
Free and full life and the consciousness
of life. Or, if you will, the pleasurable
exercise of our energies and the
enjoyment of the rest which that
exercise or expenditure of energy
makes necessary to us. I think that is
happiness for all, and covers all the difference of capacity from the most
energetic to the laziest. Now whatever
interferes with that freedom and
fullness of life, under whatever species
guise it may come, is an evil; is something to be got rid of as speedily as
possible. It ought not to be endured by
reasonable men [and women], who
naturally wish
to be happy.
—William Morris
*The Society of the Future*

It is amazing that you get so bent out of shape about social intrusiveness that can't be motivated by jealousy or inequality while you so easily tolerate inequality, advertising, competition, and alienation. You live in a society built on everyone being motivated by busybody information about one another...

CENT: But you think everyone should consume the same.

PE: The value of what every citizen consumes would be roughly equal. But what's in the equal bundle we each get will vary greatly from person to person...

CAP: What incentive is there to work?

PE: Yes, you can't get rich, though you can work harder to get more. But you are right, material incentives play a minimal role in our system. The incentive to work well is to fulfill your responsibilities and earn social esteem.

CENT: And you expect that to be sufficient? Sometimes I start to listen to you, but then you say something so absurd I wonder why I bother listening to what you have to say on any subject.

PE: Do you claim material rewards are good incentives given all you know about what they lead to? We make them an incentive of last resort. To do otherwise is what should be considered absurd. Besides would you rather go to a participatory economic doctor or to one taking time out from golf who asks for your payment before you even take off your coat?...

CAP: If your doctors spend half their time cleaning toilets and your hospitals have incompetent mediocrities doing surgery, yes, I'd rather go to my money-crazy doctors...

PE: I never proposed incompetent surgery, but you changed the subject. We were talking about incentives, not job complexes, and the reason qualitative rewards don't operate well in nonpar-ticipatory economies is because it is a rare person who is able to reject material concerns when the rest of society is propelled by greed.

MARK: You aren't going to convince any of us about this until you make the difference between your allocation system and ours clear. And I, for one, doubt you can do that. But regarding consumption, you distinguish between consumption decisions that affect a few and those that affect many. I don't disagree. We need a collective approach to public goods, but why not leave matters affecting only individuals to the marketplace? By forcing all decisions to undergo public scrutiny you will overload the circuits and won't get quality deliberation about what matters most.

CENT: But then why have consumption councils at all?

PE: You conveniently overlook that to varying degrees all goods are public. Whatever I consume affects me, but as a citizen and as a worker my behavior affects those around me as well. Of course, my consumption of particular types of food or of certain music is less "public" than my community's consumption of a new park, but nothing is ever entirely private. We need to preserve individual rights while allowing collective assessment. The idea that too little attention will be given the most important matters in a participatory economy is ironic coming from advocates of economies where almost no time goes to the most important matters, at least the most important matters to the well being of nonelite citizens. And, anyhow, how much energy goes into assessing one collective project or another, one bit of research or another, is, in participatory economics, a function of the extent of public concern and controversy about the issues themselves.

CENT: So, why not have a central planner take care of oversight and let people do their thing? Why force the sheriff role on everyone?

PE: Being concerned about collective well-being is not being a sheriff. And central planners obstruct participation. Central planning isolates people from one another and propels elite rule. The best means to integrate personal and public choices is…

MARK: With a market…

PE: No, with networks of consumer councils.

CAP: To me you are arguing over trivia. But I just can't see how people will function as you describe. If what we get is unrelated to what we do, why won't people grab all they can?

PE: There are income constraints on people's requests. You can't grab all that you might want. But even if budgets didn't provide limits, given that equitable access to goods and services is assured, why would people sacrifice friendship and respect just to salt away belongings they cannot use? Remember specific choices are anonymous, but quantity isn't. So if solidarity didn't prevent such gluttony, avoiding ostracism would. In a society where one doesn't have to fear being exploited and can't "enjoy" being rich, people won't want to pursue goodies at the risk of the human rewards that accrue from having a wide circle of friends. In any event, budgets tied to effort preclude gluttony.

CENT: But how can everyone's consumption be assured? You ignore scarcity. Of course things work out nicely in utopias…

PE: Rubbish. I didn't say everyone could have everything they might ask for. Quite the contrary, in participatory economies not only are there resource, time, and energy constraints, as in any other economy, but long before these operate workers will balk at producing more goods whose diminishing utility would be negligible compared to the human and social costs of working more. All I'm saying is people won't have to worry about becoming unemployed, losing their income, or being left behind in a scramble for wealth and status. What I get will keep up with what everyone else gets.

Anyway, whether you agree with my predictions or not, there is no point in worrying about over-consumption since participatory economies have means of oversight. In advanced capitalism rough-

The only possible alternative to being either the oppressed or the oppressor is voluntary cooperation for the greatest good of all.

—Errico Maletesta
*Volonta*, 1913

That which ordinary men are fit for, I am qualified in, and the best of me is diligence.

—Shakespeare
*King Lear*

To recapitulate: in a complex industrial economy the interrelation between its parts can be based in principle either on freely chosen negotiated contracts (which means autonomy and a species of commodity production) or on a system of binding instructions from planning offices. There is no third way.
—Alec Nove
*The Economics of Feasible Socialism*

ly 10% of consumers over-consume obscenely, 20% over-consume mightily, 30% under-consume somewhat, and 40% under-consume to the point of impaired health. In participatory economies, everyone will consume fairly.

CENT: It sounds good, but it presumes coordinating millions of consumers and hundreds of thousands of shops without planners...

MARK: Or markets to coordinate all the activities automatically...

CENT: ...in a way that allows everyone to participate. I find it inconceivable.

PE: Absolutely right. The core of my claim for participatory economics is in the possibility of a new kind of allocation that can operate effectively alongside participatory production and consumption. After all, I said that to eliminate oppressive hierarchies we must have a workplace that embodies equitable job complexes and full participation, but I have also claimed that this is impossible with markets or central planning. And I have argued for consumer councils where citizens can take into account workers' efforts and needs, and within which people can be free from the need to compete. But this, too, is impossible with markets that require competition or with central planning that precludes participation.

So, now, finally, we must discuss allocation.

# —5—

# Allocation Without Hierarchy

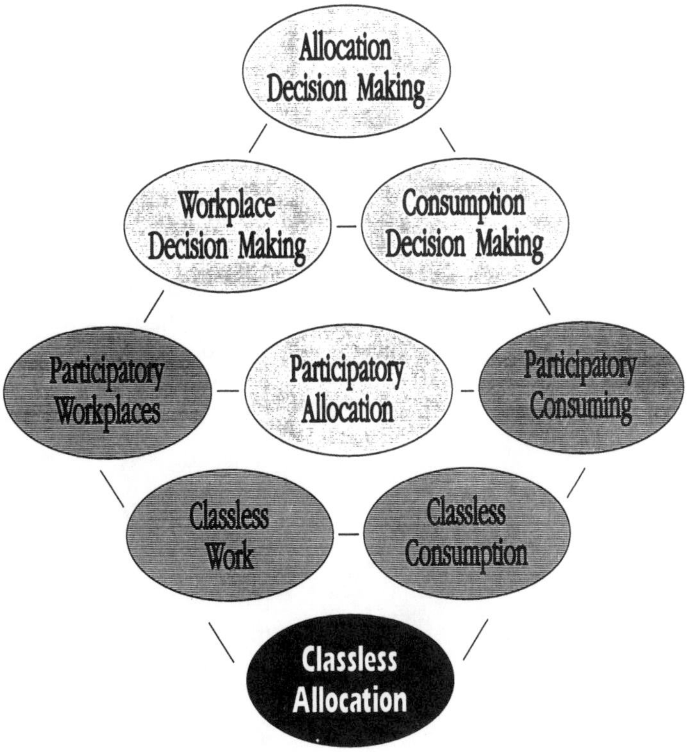

*Concepts which have proved useful for ordering things easily assume so great an authority over us, that we forget their terrestrial origin and accept them as unalterable facts. The road of scientific progress is frequently blocked for long periods by such errors.*

—Albert Einstein

**M**ost economists say economies must be based on inequality *or* coercion, competition *or* regimentation, and competitive markets *or* authoritarian planning. Why do they believe this? Why do we think they are wrong?

## Arguments Against Equity, Variety, and Participation

### Inequality or Coercion

Why do people work? Economists agree that if hard work leads to prosperity, people will work hard. "Work hard to enjoy!"

"OK, I'll work hard."

But what if paying hard-working garbage collecters, dishwashers, and miners more than layabout property owners and professionals is politically unacceptable? If society refuses to pay high wages for disagreeable work, how can it get people to collect garbage, wash dishes, or mine coal?

Economists respond that people will work hard not only to prosper, but also if it's the only way to survive. Societies unwilling to pay high wages for disagreeable work can get people to do dirty

Our present civilization has, by disinheriting millions, made the belly the center of the universe.
—Alexander Berkman

or dangerous tasks for low pay by reducing people to such desperate conditions that they welcome onerous jobs even if they also have to suffer low pay. "Work hard or suffer!"

"OK, I'll work hard."

And if that's not enough? Economists say if the threat of deprivation isn't sufficient motivation, a powerful central authority can set work norms and punish noncompliance. "Work hard or else!"

"OK, I'll work hard."

With a forlorn smile, economists conclude their discourse on motivation by letting us know that that's all there is. They proclaim Economists' Common Sense Claim #1: Other than in war time when people may pitch in spontaneously, to motivate work the only alternative to material incentives is coercion.

### Competition or Regimentation

But how do things get allocated? Economists insist there are only two viable ways to coordinate the production and consumption of millions of different goods and services in millions of separate production and consumption "units." Producers and consumers can submit to a regimented central-planning authority, or to the competitive discipline of markets, or to some of both. But, as Alec Nove puts it in his book *The Economics of Feasible Socialism* (Allen and Unwin, 1983), "there is no third way." Thus we have Economists' Common Sense Claim #2: Bureaucratic or market allocation are the only allocation options for modern economies.

### Experts and Instrumentalism

Whatever combination of inequality or coercion and competition or regimentation society chooses, certainly we also need to know who will decide what to produce and how to produce it?

Our economist friend replies: "You wonder how much of this or that to produce, how much to consume and invest, and what technologies to use. These decisions require experts. And not just scientists and engineers, but economic experts, whether central planners or investment bankers." Why? "Because economic experts are the only ones who can intelligently reduce the myriad of factors relevant to decisions to a single bottom line. Every goal must be quantified and all assets treated as instruments to be manipulated by people trained in the science of economics." And so we have Economists' Common Sense Claim #3: Decision making must be left to experts using quantitative criteria.

### Economic Wisdom or Self-Serving Ideology

Competition, inequality, coercion, and experts are facts of economic life unless we want to forgo the benefits of a division of labor

---

...We must pretend to ourselves and to everyone that fair is foul and foul is fair; for foul is useful and fair is not. Avarice and usury and persuasion must be our gods for a little longer still. For only they can lead us out of the tunnel of economic necessity into daylight.
—John Maynard Keynes

It is a far, far better thing to have a firm anchor in nonsense than to put out on the troubled seas of thought.
—John Kenneth Galbraith
*The Affluent Society*

and return to a state of nature. According to economists this is common sense. Not great news, but important for the rest of us to understand so we won't run off to try to do impossible things that will lead to disaster. It is common sense. We cannot have material well-being *and* promote solidarity, variety, and self-management. "Work hard and suffer inequality so we don't all starve."

"OK, I'll work hard."

Obviously, if we accepted Economic Common Sense claims 1, 2, and 3 we wouldn't bother trying to design a participatory economy. But we think people can coordinate their economic activities *without* competition or regimentation, be motivated to work *without* gross inequalities or coercion, and make insightful, humane decisions *without* being dominated by experts of any kind. What supports these optimistic claims in the face of the sage admonitions of the high priests of the "dismal science," economics?

Imagine a railroad baron who claimed in 1850 that the "laws of transport" ruled out travel by air. The baron could not offer a scientific proof of his claim, but only overwhelming data showing that no one had ever flown. We know by hindsight that his argument committed the fallacy of "unimaginative projection."

Today, economists offer even more sweeping claims with no more support than that *the facts of contemporary life* accord with their pessimistic projections. Just as the facts of urban congestion once supported an incorrect projection, economists repeat a modern version of the fallacy of unimaginative projection when they label contemporary personality types inevitable products of human nature and argue that solidarity is impossible.

It's true that allocation institutions strongly influence what we produce and consume. Indeed, to understand why contemporary facts seem to accord with economists' pessimistic claims we need only note that *both* markets and central planning deny workers information about the situation of consumers and other workers and subordinate workers to powers beyond their reach. Both divide the work force into task masters and task doers and rely on material incentives and coercion. Both create competition, regimentation, inequality, coercion, experts, and instrumental decision making.

Our problem is therefore to devise a way to carry out economic allocation efficiently while promoting equity, solidarity, variety, and collective self-management. To begin doing this we first consider information and communication.

*"Competition, inequality, coercion, and experts are facts of economic life unless we want to forgo the benefits of a division of labor and return to a state of nature."*

Now the problem arises of how to unite freedom and organization; how to combine mastery of the workers over the work with the binding up of all this work in a well-planned social entirety. How to organize production, in every shop as well as over the whole of world economy, in such a way that they themselves as parts of a collaborating community regulate their work.
—Anton Pannekoek

## Contours of Economic Allocation

### *Participatory Communication*

It would be utopian to assume that people always knew where "society's interest" lay and could be relied on to advance it. If we assume that everyone always understands and considers "society's

The Lord of the Flies hung in space before him. "What are you doing out here all alone? Aren't you afraid of me?" Simon shook. "There isn't anyone to help you. Only me. And I'm the beast." Simon's mouth labored, brought forth audible words. "Pig's head on a stick."
—William Goldman
*Lord of the Flies*

interest," we will have assumed away all problems even before any human actor has appeared.

But having avoided the temptation to solve all problems by assuming all people are omniscient and saintly, we should also avoid assuming that everyone is necessarily myopic and greedy. Taking into account social costs and benefits when reasonable estimates are provided is a far cry from miraculously knowing "society's interest." Moreover, in a context that promotes solidarity, there is every reason to expect that people may come to care about one another.

With this established, we can ask what participatory economic actors need to know to make sensible allocation decisions that promote solidarity, variety, and collective self management.

A critical insight is that everything has an "opportunity cost." Anything we do will use time, energy, and resources that we cannot use for something else. Proposing $x$, how can we know that the results will be better than applying the same means to doing $y$ instead? That is, the production of any good entails "social opportunity costs" that are important to know if we are to regulate production and consumption proportionately to its effects on ourselves, our co-workers, and consumers.

First, as a participatory worker you need to know how the goods you produce will be used and how much people need them. For example, to decide how hard you want to work and what technologies to use, you need to weigh the relative gains from working less, or from employing technologies that are more fulfilling but less productive, against the needs and desires of people you produce for. Clearly, you can't get this information from knowing only the gross amount of money anonymous consumers of unequal income will pay for your product.

Second, you need some basis for determining an equitable, an above-average, and a below-average allocation of work effort. You need to know the average effort contributed by each worker in your industry and workplace, and in society as a whole.

Third, as a participatory consumer, to act responsibly you need to know what is a reasonable, greedy, or overly frugal demand, and you have to be able to balance gains to yourself or your family, neighborhood, or region against the costs of providing what you seek. What allocation procedures can provide all this information?

Under capitalism, markets reduce information to manipulative advertising and to prices that misrepresent true social costs and benefits. This precludes solidarity and promotes control by experts or capitalists. In centrally-planned economies, there is no democratic circulation of quantitative or qualitative information. Central authorities determine what is to be known and what isn't as well as who is to know and who isn't. Even local council structures won't promote self-management and solidarity if allocation institutions deny council members the means to intelligently express their preferences and weigh them against the preferences of others. Assume, for example, that workers and consumers are organized into councils but that these councils are coordinated by competitive

*"...you need some basis for determining an equitable, an above average, and a below-average allocation of work effort. You need to know the average effort contributed by each worker in your industry and workplace, and in society as a whole."*

markets. Each council understands only its own situation and the prices for which things can be bought and sold. Since market prices misestimate social costs and benefits (due to ubiquitous "external effects" which impact on people beyond immediate buyers and sellers), the first problem is that market prices do not provide best estimates of the true social costs and benefits to others of the things council members request or supply. The second problem is that even if market prices accurately estimated true social costs and benefits, with no further *qualitative* information about the conditions that create the human costs and benefits for others, people do not have the necessary information to develop empathy and come to consider others' interests as they do their own. Third, in a competitive market environment workers and consumers councils would have no incentive to consider the interests of others. To survive in a competitive market environment there is only an incentive to take maximum advantage of those from whom one buys and to whom one sells. To behave differently is self defeating.

In other words, the information and incentive properties of markets prevent even democratic councils from considering the well-being of others in making decisions. As a result, council members in market systems sensibly leave technical decisions to expert decision makers (what we call the coordinator class), as in Yugoslavia. In contrast, in participatory economies, we need allocation institutions that can successfully communicate socially relevant and accurate information and also make it in the interest of every council to further the interests of others. Then collective self-management will be both possible and sensible.

For "participatory accounting" the economy must therefore provide information allowing producers and consumers to reason effectively about their own needs and how they fit with everyone else's. A central task of participatory allocation is therefore to provide information sufficient for self management without rendering decision making excessively time consuming. One tool to this end is to *adapt* the use of prices and money by altering the definition of each.

In sum, the workers fight over bread, they snatch mouthfuls from each other, one is the enemy of the rest, because each searches solely for his [sic] own well-being without bothering about the well-being of the rest; and this antagonism between individuals of the same class, this deaf struggle for miserable crumbs, makes our slavery permanent, perpetuates misery, causes our misfortunes—because we don't understand that the interest of our neighbor is our own interest, because we sacrifice ourselves for a poorly understood individual interest, searching in vain for well-being which can only be the result of our interest in the matters which affect all humanity.
—Ricardo Flores Magon
*Speech in El Monte, California, 1917*

## Socially Planned Indicative Prices and Accounting Money

Imagine that you want to buy a typewriter and have material goods but no money. Bartering furniture for a typewriter would be needlessly complicated. If the person with the typewriter doesn't like your furniture, or doesn't want furniture at all, it may require a three, four, or many party trade to accomplish what monetary exchange could facilitate with minimal inconvenience.

Yet in a capitalist society, money plays an additional role. Individuals with wealth can use it to expropriate part of what others produce. This can take many more or less transparent forms, but when those who do little or no work often live far better than those

*"For "participatory accounting" the economy must therefore provide information allowing producers and consumers to reason effectively about their own needs and how they fit with everyone else's."*

I never would believe that Providence
had sent a few rich men into the world,
ready booted and spurred to ride, and
millions ready saddled and
bridled to be ridden.
—Richard Rumbold
*Statement on scaffold before being
hung for rebellion, 1685*

Money doesn't talk. It swears.
—Bob Dylan
*Liner Notes*

who shoulder the burdens of social labor there can be no doubt that
money can be not only socially beneficial by facilitating exchange
but also socially detrimental as a vehicle for exploitation. Moreover, since market demand is measured in quantity of dollars spent
which in turn determines what is produced, in market economies
members of different classes exert disproportionate influence on
production. Thus, there is nothing democratic about "consumer
sovereignty" when there is an unequal distribution of wealth.

It follows from this that in a participatory economy, while we
want the convenience that prices and money offer, we do not want
the associated ill effects. We want producers and consumers to be
able to determine the social costs and benefits of different commodities, and we want producers and consumers to be able to
distinguish reasonable from overly-frugal and overly-greedy consumption requests, and we want convenient transactions. But we
do not want decisions to be based solely on reductionist accounting.

Likewise, since there is no more reason to insist that people's
consumption match their effort in a given year than in a given day,
we want people to be free to arrange the timing of what they give
and take from society to their own convenience as much as possible.
That is, we want people to be able to save or borrow and to work
harder or less hard to get greater or lesser purchasing power at
different times in their lives. We therefore want something like
money to facilitate participatory decision making and exchange—
but we do not want to introduce the exploitative evils of capital.
Likewise, we want something like prices to facilitate social planning by allowing comparisons of different goods, and also something like income to allow us to compare the overall social burden
proposed by different consumption bundles. But we do not want to
substitute reductionist measures for social assessments of the
human dimensions of work and consumption.

Typical market prices fluctuate because of bargaining by large
corporations (seeking increased profits), unions and workers (seeking better wages and working conditions), and consumers (seeking
a better deal). Moreover, advertising, monopoly, and government
policies also affect prices. In a participatory economy, in contrast,
we want "prices" to reflect only the true social costs and benefits
of goods including scarce resources used, other products needed as
inputs, work efforts, and positive and negative byproducts such as
pollution and changes in producers' and consumers' skill levels,
personalities, and social relations.

We will argue that the participatory "prices" generated by the
social, iterative procedure we call participatory allocation reflect
true preferences, technological constraints, and resource limitations far more accurately than do market prices. But even though
participatory prices are more accurate than competitive market
prices, we do not want to become overly dependent on quantitative
indicators in place of a richer, qualitative understanding of social
relations. Even if accurate participatory prices could be generated
without a social assessment of all the material, human, and social
factors associated with production and consumption, we would not

want to reduce our decision making to calculating a numerical bottom line. This would diminish our sensitivity to our fellow workers and to the intricate tapestry of human activities that determine what we can and cannot consume or produce. Moreover, due to tendencies of prices to increasingly diverge from accuracy unless they are periodically socially updated, we cannot preserve accurate participatory prices without a periodic qualitative social assessment of all the factors involved in production and consumption. We thus need accurate indicative prices that reflect insights gleaned from periodic qualitative social evaluations.

Similarly, though "money" in our participatory society must allow workers to earn more (or less) now for a greater (or lesser) work effort, and consumers to purchase more (or less) now by borrowing on future rights (or saving for a future of greater need), it must not distort balanced job complexes or yield inequities in the form of some people living off the labor of others. To remind ourselves that participatory prices and money are similar to their capitalist counterparts in only some respects and that we will take pains to strip them of their exploitative and reductionist characteristics, we will call them "indicative" or participatory prices and "accounting" money. Indicative prices in the sense that they indicate the social costs and benefits of things as accurately as we can, and accounting money to emphasize that money is only a measuring tool.

> The great are great only because we are on our knees. Let us rise!
> —Max Stirner
> *The Ego and His Own*

## *Measuring Work Expended*

We have said we want workers to be able to overwork to make above-average purchases or to make below-average purchases and underwork. In an earlier chapter, we also clarified that we did not want class differences to evolve between people doing work complexes with markedly different effects. We urged that whenever a plant had above-average conditions, its workers would spend some time doing more menial tasks elsewhere, and that whenever a plant had below-average conditions the workers would spend time in more interesting pursuits elsewhere. The idea was that everybody's work be balanced regarding demands and rewards even while differing in particular characteristics.

In this context, for an individual to work nonaverage hours in a given period and not disrupt a humane balance of job complexes, he or she could diminish or increase his or her hours worked at all tasks in the same proportion. Each individual could then receive from his or her workplace an indicator of average labor hours expended as an accurate indicator of work effort contributed. Over a sufficient period, whenever a person's indicator was high (low) compared to the social average, the individual would have contributed more (less) to the social product and would be entitled to ask for more (less) consumption now or at some later date. Accounting money income thus equates to *real* socially average labor hours

> *"Indicative prices in the sense that they indicate the social costs and benefits of things as accurately as we can, and accounting money to emphasize that money is only a measuring tool."*

It is critical to realize that *unlike* in any other kind of economy, since job balancing actually occurs in our system, socially average hours are a real and measurable concept in a participatory economy. We should also remember that in a participatory economy one's consumption depends not only on one's work effort but also on one's needs. If you request above-average consumption because of some ailment or personal project approved by your neighborhood council and producers, you don't necessarily have to work more or borrow to receive it. Work expended plays a pivotal role, however, when a person wants to consume above average in ways others would not OK. Participatory economics does not rule out some people working harder to consume more nor consuming more because of special approved needs. But participatory economics does rule out some people consuming more than others without working more or having special needs.

Still, what enables people to understand the details of one another's situations, as we have said they will?

> Toleration is not the opposite of intoleration, but is the counterfeit of it. Both are despotisms. The one assumes to itself the right of withholding liberty of conscience, and the other of granting it. The one is Pope armed with fire and fagot, and the other is the Pope selling or granting indulgences.
> —Thomas Paine
> *The Rights of Man*

## *Qualitative Description*

We have said we would like producers to respect the needs and desires of the people they produce for and consumers to respect the sacrifices of the people who produce what they consume. To facilitate this, we certainly want economic actors to have easy access to indicative prices summarizing large amounts of information. But these prices should *only* be facilitators.

However odd it may initially appear, what participatory economics requires to prevent reductionist accounting is for each actor to have access to a list of everything that goes into producing goods she or he consumes, and everything that results from the goods she or he produces. Of course, not all of this vast store of qualitative information will be used by every worker and consumer in every decision—there would be too much even to read. But we contend that over time people will become familiar with the "congealed components" of products they regularly use, just as they are now familiar with the products themselves. Then, whenever consumers ask producers to meet a high demand, or producers ask consumers to lower demands so that workers can enjoy a more leisurely work life, each party will be able to consider the qualitative dimensions of the other's requests.

For example, as a worker, if I am considering improving the quality of work, I need to know what dislocations any reorganization will cause consumers so I can weigh their discomfort against my gains. As a consumer, I need to know the human costs of producing the goods I desire so as to be able to weigh the benefit to me against the costs to others. Do I want to backoff and lower my request, or do I want to maintain it and argue that either workers should produce more or someone else should cut *their* demand?

*"Participatory economics does not rule out some people working harder to consume more or consuming more because of special approved needs. But participatory economics does rule out some people consuming more than others without working more or having special needs."*

While these calculations could be based solely on participatory indicative prices, we contend that these would become inaccurate if people didn't also pay attention to qualitative details (for a detailed proof of this claim see *Quiet Revolution in Welfare Economics*, Princeton University Press). In any case, certainly the empathetic and social character of deciding economic activities would deteriorate if *only* indicative prices were used. People must have access to information about actual conditions of production as well as about gains expected from consumption.

If an individual seeks an unusually expensive consumption bundle, he or she will have to justify the request to his or her consumption council to have it OK'd as part of the council's proposal. If the council's request is above the per capita average and producers balk at producing more, the council must decide whether to lower its request in the next planning round, or to hold out in expectation that other councils will lower their requests or that workers will offer to raise production. To make these types of decisions, both producers and consumers must have ready access not only to summary price data, but to detailed qualitative accounts. Only this will ensure that the human and social dimension of economic decision making isn't lost and thereby guarantee that summary price data remains accurate.

Still, suppose I want to consume more computers. The computer factory uses chips made at a chip factory, which in turn uses machinery made at a machine factory. Do I have to know all this information—the impact of my request on all these factories? To see, we have to examine the role of various allocation institutions in chapter 6. Then we will be able to see how information would actually be used and decisions made in some hypothetical workplaces and living units in chapters 7 and 8.

Can I see another's woe,
And not be in sorrow too?
Can I see another's grief,
And not seek for kind relief?
—William Blake
*On Another's Sorrow*

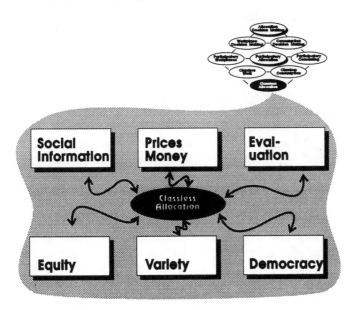

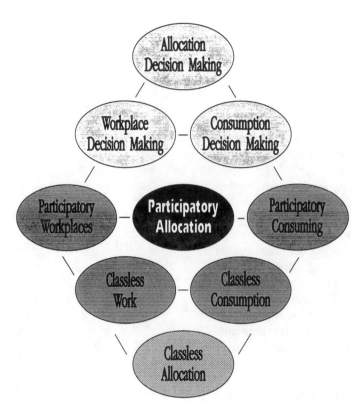

# 6

# Participatory Allocation

*Annual income twenty pounds, annual expenditure nineteen nineteen six, result happiness. Annual income twenty pounds, annual expenditure twenty pounds ought and six, result misery.*

—Charles Dickens

The basic actors in participatory planning are workers' and consumers' councils that allow ordinary citizens to make decisions about production in their workplaces and about their personal and neighborhood consumption. But besides neighborhood consumers' councils, we also have ward, city, county, state, and regional councils responsible for summing the proposals of lower levels and adding collective requests. And beside workplace councils, we have regional and industry council federations.

In addition, Consumption Facilitation Boards (CFBs) operate at different consumption levels to assess issues such as collective consumption proposals, and Production Facilitation Boards (PFBs) operate at different levels to consider issues such as production externalities and economies of scale. Employment Facilitation Boards (EFBs) assist workers in changing their places of employment and Household Facilitation Boards (HFBs) help citizens find membership in communities and neighborhoods.

Additionally, at every level we find Updating Facilitation Boards (UFBs) responsible for facilitating the least disruptive methods of updating planning requests to take account of unforeseen circumstances. And finally, to facilitate convergence of the planning process we also have Iteration Facilitation Boards (IFBs).

To participate, each consumption actor proposes a plan for the upcoming period. Individuals request private goods for the year. Neighborhood or other collective consumption units sum personal requests and develop collective consumption requests as well.

Similarly, each production actor proposes a plan for the upcoming period. Whether the actor is an individual, work group, workplace, or industry the proposal lists the inputs needed to complete the proposed activities and the outputs that will result.

Of course, the collection of first proposals for consumption and production will not be equal, or in economist's jargon, first proposals will not comprise a feasible plan. The initial demand for most goods will exceed proposed supply.

In any event, after receiving information regarding the proposals of all other actors and other actors' reactions to one's own initial proposal, each actor makes a new new proposal. In time, as actors "bargain" with one another through successive "iterations" (or rounds of bargaining), the process converges to an implementable plan. No central agency composes the final plan. No market competition generates the final plan. A decentralized, social, iterative, communication process allows all actors to democratically *formulate* the final plan.

But how does anybody know what to propose? Why won't bargaining continue forever. Moreover, even if the planning process converges to a feasible conclusion, what will guarantee that it will be efficient and equitable, and what will ensure that people can save or borrow as they choose? And what if desires or circumstances alter during the year? Will we be bound to do whatever we said on January 1 even when July rolls around and we are unexpectedly ill? Or what if workers encounter unexpected problems? How can anyone offer a responsible accounting of what he or she will consume or produce for a whole year?

For the moment, let's *assume* the system has been in operation for many years and ask what a planning process for a new year would be like under such conditions. This will let us answer the above questions, and though it sidesteps important difficulties of transition from current procedures and habits, we can worry about transition after we're convinced there is something worth "transitioning" to.

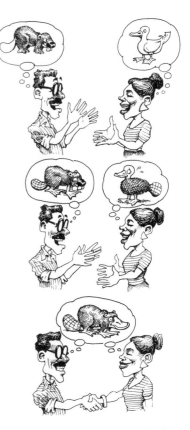

*"No central agency composes the final plan. No market competition generates the final plan. A decentralized, social, iterative, communication process allows all actors to democratically formulate the final plan."*

## Preparing First Proposals

Last year our economy carried out various acts of production and consumption that constituted "plans" for individuals, consumption councils, workplaces, and industries. As this year begins we have records of all these "plans." We also know last year's final indicative prices and per capita consumption, as well as the average ratio of social benefit to social cost for workplaces last year. Additionally, each unit knows how it altered its proposals during last year's planning process, moderating its own requests in light of other's needs. Similarly, each unit has access to the same data for the history of any other unit's transactions.

Readers who think we are beginning to write science fiction should know that contemporary database systems are already sufficiently powerful to sustain this kind of information storage, manipulation, and retrieval. A few major credit companies *now possess and regularly use* substantial data files on tens of millions

In the U.S. in 1988 there were 91 million households with an average of 2.69 members. Regarding consumer outlets, in 1986 there were, for example, 187,430 food stores, 362,895 eating and drinking places, 36,037 general merchandise stores, 141,884 apparel and accessory stores, 205,597 real estate offices, 54,759 banks, 18,543 movie theaters, and 2,018 museums.

of consumers which approaches the level required to describe and record the various economic operations we want to track. Regarding the task of bringing everyone into communication with this data, we already have a comprehensive phone network, and the only thing needed to establish a fully interactive hookup is unlimited distribution of computer terminals and phone accessories called modems. Produced on the scale we require, cost per participant could drop as low as a hundred dollars or less for units that would last many years. Similarly, memory storage and operating capacity are growing so fast that technical means of accommodating participatory planning will surely exist before social demand for such a system matures.

So how does an individual consumer or worker plan? First we obtain relevant data about last year's plan. Second, we receive information from various Iteration Facilitation Boards (IFBs) about anticipated indicative prices, income, and value of product that should be attained per value of input used (benefit-to-cost ratio) this year, all arrived at by adapting last year's final figures in light of investment decisions and changes in the work force and consumer population. Third, we receive information from higher-level production and consumption councils and from production and consumption facilitation boards regarding major investments agreed to as part of long-run planning and their implications for the present.

Finally, taking into account our intended work levels and any borrowing or saving we are planning, we develop a personal consumption proposal for the coming year. Assuming the eventual result will be equitable, our proposal is implicitly our "vote" for the average consumption the economy should have, and, by way of the fact that all this must be produced, also the average amount of work we think people should do. Similarly, our work proposal implies what we think the average work effort should be and therefore what society's total production and consumption should be. In short, in making an initial personal proposal each actor proposes their own consumption and production but also, implicitly an average and overall workload, and an average and overall level of consumption. In fact, each individual implicitly proposes all this twice, once in their personal consumption proposal and once in their personal work proposal.

But does this mean we must itemize every single good down to size and color? No, because IFBs group goods into classes according as they are roughly interchangeable regarding the resources, intermediate goods, and labor required to produce them. So we need only choose from among types of goods. Similarly, we don't bother with sizes or colors, since demographic data allows producers to extrapolate within an acceptable range of error from total requests say, for 7 million sneakers, to more precise demands for so many size 8, so many size 9, and so many of each style and color.

*"Similarly, our personal work proposal implies what we think the average work effort should be and therefore what society's total production and consumption should be."*

As an individual, therefore, you present your consumption request to your neighborhood council. where it is summed with others. Neighborhood collective consumption requests are added to form the neighborhood council's complete request which is submitted to the ward council where a similar process ensues, on up to the national consumption council.

In the same way, workers access a summary of the history of their proposals last year including the initial proposal, changes made during planning iterations, what was finally agreed on, and also what was actually carried out if there was any discrepancy. IFBs also provide estimates of what changes in demand are likely this year based on extrapolations from demographic data and last year's demands before they were reduced during iterations.

Workers consider this information, discuss their own desires, and enter work proposals which are assembled into the workers' council's first proposal for "inputs" and "outputs" by procedures we discuss next chapter.

In addition, both workers' and consumers' councils provide qualitative addenda to their proposals, including descriptions of changes in their circumstances and conditions. If the quality of work in a workplace has altered due to previous investments that have reduced noise or made surroundings more agreeable, it would be noted. Similarly, if the purpose for which a consumer council requests a good is different from last year, this too would be noted. However, when we say units would assemble information and make their proposals available, we do not mean they trudge around searching for data and send off copies of proposals to every unit in the country. Planning is computerized. All councils can access data banks of all facilitation boards and all other councils. The only thing demanding about flexible information access is that the computer system not only automatically accept but also sum and compare proposals to ascertain the status of any good—which brings us to the problem of "planning iterations."

*"Workers desiring goods to enact improvements request them. Workers at plants producing the goods requested decide whether they wish to provide them. The dynamic is like any other consumer/producer interaction."*

## Going from One Proposal to Another

First proposals are in. We have all answered how much and in what form we think we want to work and consume under an optimistic assessment of possibilities. Are we ready to call the resulting aggregate a plan, or must we have another round?

To decide we sum all consumption requests and all production proposals and compare demand with supply for every class of good. In the first iteration or round, when consumers are supposed to propose ambitious consumption bundles and workers are supposed to propose desirable work plans, for most goods demand exceeds supply which means everyone's initial proposals cannot be simultaneously implemented. In planning terminology, the initial proposals do not yield a feasible plan and the status of most goods is in excess demand by some percentage.

Next, every council receives new data regarding the degree to which goods it offered or requested were in excess supply or excess demand and how its requests compared with those of other units. Did my workplace council offer to produce less than other similar

*"The changed indicative prices in turn provide councils new estimates of the social costs and benefits of different items they request or offer to produce."*

*"With each new iteration, the fact that goods previously in excess demand will have a higher price when councils next decide how much they want and that goods previously in excess supply will have a lower price, will create a new context for decision making."*

production units; did my consumers' council request a bundle larger than others' consumption requests?

IFBs translate excess demands and any excess supplies into appropriate changes in the "indicative" prices for those goods by raising the prices of goods in excess demand and lowering the prices of goods in excess supply, with greater changes the higher the percent of excess demand or supply. The changed indicative prices in turn provide councils new estimates of the social costs and benefits of different items they request or offer to produce.

Next since councils must eventually win the approval of other councils for their proposals, consumers' councils are under "peer" pressure to bring their overall consumption requests into line with average per capita consumption, and workers' councils are under "peer" pressure to bring the ratio of the social benefits of their outputs to the social costs of their inputs up to the national average. But this does not mean that every consumer council must consume the average amount of every item, or that every workplace in an industry must use inputs in the same proportions to make their output. By multiplying the amount of each good requested by its "indicative" price and summing on its computer terminals, each consumers' council can compare the average per member value of its requests to the average per member value of other councils' requests and to the national average. Of course, in the participatory economy "overall value" of a consumption request is just another way of saying the "overall burden on scarce resources and laboring capacities" that a consumption request places on the rest of the economy. Likewise, by multiplying outputs by their indicative prices and summing to attain the total value of products (social benefit), and multiplying inputs by their indicative prices and summing to attain the total value of inputs used (social cost), each workers' council can calculate its own social benefit to social cost ratio for comparison to the ratios of other workplaces and industry- and economy-wide averages.

With each new round of planning, goods previously in excess demand will have a higher price when councils next decide how much they want and that goods previously in excess supply will have a lower price. These changed prices will create a new context for decision making. Councils will usually revise proposals first by substituting inputs whose indicative prices have fallen for inputs whose indicative prices have risen, and for workplaces, substituting outputs whose indicative prices have risen for outputs whose prices have fallen. These *shifting* adjustments will promote economic efficiency and alleviate the extent to which individual councils must engage in the other kind of proposal revision, *reducing* adjustments. But if after making shifting adjustments, the value of a consumption request remains higher than the national average, and if work effort proposals and borrowing/saving plans do not justify the excess, and if no special circumstances are deemed to warrant the excess, and if there is no expectation in the consumers' council that circumstances in coming iterations will change in favor of the council, then the council will feel pressure to *reduce* its overall request to bring its per-member value into line with the national average. And, likewise, if after shifting adjustments a workers' council still cannot generate an acceptable excess of social benefits over social costs, and if it has no viable excuse (such a greater need) and no sensible expectation that conditions will change in its favor in the following iteration, it will feel pressure to increase its work effort. Moreover, as the rounds of planning proceed, price indicators will begin to approach their final resting places and consumers and workers will have less justification for "holding out" in overly expensive consumption requests or insufficient production offerings expecting new prices to ratify their stance. Ultimately a workplace unable to sufficiently improve its ratio of social benefits to social costs might even be asked to disperse, since it is not in society's interest to permit resources that could be used more productively elsewhere to be used unproductively in such a unit.

In the above summary, the essential logic of proposal revision is straightforward: peer review backed by the necessity of getting one's proposal accepted pressures actors to bring their consumption and work proposals "into line," so that people contribute efforts commensurate to the efforts they implicitly demand from others. Ever more accurate estimates of social costs and benefits of goods induce workers and consumers to shift from goods in greater excess demand to goods in greater excess supply thereby promoting the social interest via an efficient allocation of scarce productive resources. Simultaneously, reductions of unacceptably expensive consumption requests or lazy production proposals are promoted. In a context where socially responsible behavior is induced, individual actors receive the information they need to reconcile their individual pursuit of well being with others' equally deserving attempts to do likewise. Differences in consumers' desires and the desires and capabilities of different workers' councils are accounted for, as well as variations in the timing of people's contributions and receipt of benefits. The pressure brought to bear on participants promotes efficiency and equity, *not* uniformity.

Each new round of planning yields a new set of proposed activities for all consumers and producers as well as new estimates of indicative prices, average consumption, and average work productivity. But what propels the process toward a conclusion that everyone will accept? How do we know the final allocation will be superior to what a central planner or market system would have arrived at? Moreover, how do we update when conditions change during the year? We'll address the last concern first, since it helps clarify how the other concerns are addressed.

*"Differences in consumers' desires and the desires and capabilities of different workers' councils are accounted for, as well as variations in the timing of people's contributions and receipt of benefits. The pressure brought to bear on participants promotes efficiency and equity, not uniformity."*

## Updating a Settled Plan

Converging and updating are related because each benefits from "tricks" that take advantage of the large scale of planning. Let's assume we have settled on a plan for the year. Why might we need to update the initially agreed on plan as the year evolves, and how might we do so?

As a consumer you begin your year with approved requests for different kinds of food, clothing, meals at restaurants, trips, gas, books, records, and tickets to performances you will consume over the year. Suppose you also have a computer "credit card" that has all this information stored in its portable memory and which records your consumptions, subtracting them from your year's allotment as you go. What if you want to change what you consume from what you planned?

You belong to a neighborhood council, which in turn belongs to a network of consumer federations. Many changes you propose may be counterbalanced by changes others propose in your neighborhood, ward, county, etc. Obviously consumption changes that cancel one another would not affect production and could be easily accommodated by consumer councils and federations.

If I want more of this and less of that, and my neighbor wants the reverse—or, more likely, if the ups and downs of three thousand of us all requesting modest changes in this, that, and the other largely cancel out—then production needn't change significantly. Even if the sum of all changes in proposed consumption of milk by all members of your neighborhood council sum to a significant increase in demand, that total may be balanced by opposite changes in other neighborhood councils so that only distribution is affected.

Sometimes, however, changes will not balance so that the net increase, say, in milk demand must be communicated to milk producers, who then either produce more—by increasing work intensity, hours worked by each employee, or adding personnel—or refuse to increase production.

Since any increase in milk production will more than likely require more inputs, there would be secondary effects whose impact may cancel out with secondary effects of adjustments in other industries, or may not. If people's consumption is recorded automatically on their "credit card" computers and deducted from their annual allocation, periodic updates could be easily communicated to relevant updating facilitation boards (UFBs) which could in turn communicate projected changes in consumer demand, first to relevant consumer federations, and then, if necessary, to relevant industry federations. In response, workers propose accommodating changes they are willing to undertake and consumers are told the relevant changes they can incorporate into their expectations. Such dialogues can certainly lead to work diminishing in some industries and increasing in others, with transfers of employees as necessary, but there would be no more moving about than in other kinds of economies and probably quite a bit less since the cost of workers having to change jobs would be a factor in the collective determination of whether to meet changed demands.

In light of the above we can see that since each council's activities have implications for others, if the matches between supply and demand are calculated too closely in the original plan,

Is a participatory planning apparatus too large to implement? In 1987 just over 3 million individuals were employed by the federal government of the United States in nonmilitary posts. (Just under 100 million was the total nonmilitary employment for the country as a whole.) The government positions include 44,000 computer specialists, 60,000 clerk typists, 18,000 lawyers, 23,000 air traffic controllers, 27,000 criminal investigators, 38,000 nurses, and so on. The executive department of the executive branch alone had over 1 million civilian employees including roughly 116,000 in agriculture, 31,000 in defense, 122,000 in health and human services, 4,500 in education, 245,000 in veterans affairs, etc. The federal court system had about 21,000 employees. Would it require more than this to maintain the planning apparatus of a participatory economy?

*"Suppose you also have a computer 'credit card' that has all this information stored in its portable memory and which records your consumptions, subtracting them from your year's allotment as you go."*

changes during the year would more likely disrupt the whole economy. There would be too much moving and debating in a network that was planned too tightly. So to simplify updating, participatory planning incorporates "slack." All industries produce more than planned demand in the first place and also plan excess capacity so they can expand output even further should the occasion arise. Likewise, the plan leaves some extra resource availability. At the same time, individuals would not be allowed to dramatically change their requests without receiving an OK from their consumption council, nor could workers in a company unduly lower output without an OK from their industry council. With these provisos, it ought to be clear that flexibly accommodating changing tastes and possibilities is not beyond the capacity of a participatory economy with appropriate "slack" built in. And before the cynical reader cries "waste," he or she should note that depending on how one measures the contemporary U.S. economy runs with between 15 percent and 25 percent unutilized capacity, and that this is easily two to three times more than what would be needed in a participatory economy.

Finally, the law of averages regarding the likelihood of proposed changes offsetting one another and a general social knowledge of those industries most likely to be affected by nonaveraging changes would allow *informed* "slack planning." During the iterative process, that is, the IFBs would propose relevant slack for various products in tune with past histories and with other variables we will discuss later. These would enter the final plan as some proportion of each unit's output and potential output that would not necessarily be produced.

## Converging

A little thought reveals there is no reason to expect a totally unguided sequence of participatory planning iterations to necessarily converge. For example, one product that begins in excess demand could flip into excess supply in the next iteration as workers offer to produce more and consumers to request less, and this flip-flop could continue from round to round. Alternatively, a good's status might not reverse every time but might follow a crazy path that never converges toward equilibrium. Moreover, when we consider that each product's status affects the status of many others, so that during an iteration changes in eating out at restaurants will affect the status of gas for cars and food for home cooking, we can see just how messy things might become. Just as we make progress on one front, another could get farther out of whack. Economists conveniently deploy simplifying assumptions to make these problems go away in their economic models—must notably what they call "convexity" and "gross substitutability" assumptions. But the only way to make these problems "go away" in the real world

*"Moreover, when we consider that each product's status affects the status of many others, so that during an iteration changes in eating out at restaurants will affect the status of gas for cars and food for home cooking, we can see just how messy things might become."*

Is it possible to move such substantial amounts of information to so many different nodes? Consider that we are talking about moving electronic information. The U.S. postal system has the much harder task of moving physical packages. In fact, in 1987 the federal postal service had nearly 840,000 employees moving roughly 160 billion pieces of mail (about 656 pieces per capita). To accomplish this there are a little over 40,000 post offices, stations, branches, and so on. Obviously a much smaller apparatus would suffice for participatory planning's communicative infrastructure—perhaps something about the size of United Parcel Services, operating a communications process more like a computer information service.

*"You suggest some level of work effort for yourself and, implicitly, an average for everyone, and some level of consumption for yourself and, again, implicitly, an average for everyone. To be realistic you make these proposals compatible."*

is to implement flexible rules and deploy experienced IFBs to help guide the process. Clearly, we need to adopt rules and authorize interventions that do not bias outcomes or reduce efficiency or equity unduly but that do ensure that convergence occurs in a reasonable time.

We should emphasize again that *there is no one correct way to operate a participatory planning system.* Many features are contingent. The various tasks we have enumerated could surely be carried out in different ways. Facilitation boards could be defined differently or even replaced by other institutions. Moreover, in real societies, economies exist in social contexts co-determined by kinship relations, governing forms, and cultural relations (as discussed further in our concluding chapter). There is no reason to expect that participatory structures will be identical despite differences in these other spheres of social life. Thus, developing preferred rules and institutions will be largely a historical task. Chosen forms in any particular society will have to fit particular environmental, historical, and cultural circumstances that no abstract model such as ours can fully anticipate, and, in any event, the character of optimal institutions and rules will alter as any particular participatory economy develops. It may even be that within one economy different but compatible rule systems will operate in different areas, reflecting differences in climate, resources, or culture. Here, therefore, we only describe *one* workable approach for getting the "bargaining process" to converge to a desirable economic plan. Even the simple approach we highlight, however, suffices to demonstrate the viability of participatory planning and illustrate the kinds of calculations and decisions essential to its operation.

The first step in our example planning process is for each individual to think about his or her plan for the year. We can save some mental energy by considering someone who is intending not to save or borrow, since savers and borrowers function identically after appropriate adjustments. Everyone works at balanced job complexes and everyone receives an updated calculation of projected averages for production and consumption before each iteration. The iteration facilitation boards (IFBs) use knowledge of last year's plan, productive investments, changes in the labor force, and estimates of necessary "slack" to predict total output and translate this into average consumption and work loads. Each individual thus has an idea of what a fair consumption request and fair work proposal would be.

Now consider making a first proposal. You suggest some level of work effort for yourself and, implicitly, an average for everyone, and some level of consumption for yourself and, again, implicitly, an average for everyone. To be realistic—after taking into account what may be your above average needs—you make these proposals compatible. Therefore, what you really propose is: "I would like to work such and such an amount at my job complex and to consume such and such a total, broken into the following particular items. My work total and consumption total generally accord with each other and assume such and such an average consumption and production for society." Everyone makes a similar proposal in light of their particular preferences and capabilities but recognizing that the overall amount consumed must be produced, and that the distribution of burdens and benefits should be equitable..

Note that it wouldn't even be possible to actually enact everyone's first production proposals, since in most workplaces one person in a team may have proposed working more hours than another person in the same team, even though they can only work together. The *plant's* first production proposal used for IFB's calculations of new indicative prices, must therefore be calculated as an abstracted average of all its workers' separate proposals. In any event, after first proposals are summed and the results tabulated and summarized the second iteration can proceed.

According to the rule system in this example economy, everyone would still act individually. You compare your proposed work load and proposed consumption with the average of others' proposals. You also consider more localized averages, for example in your workplace, industry, complex, or neighborhood. You consider the status of each item you ordered and consult explanations of what seemed to be oddities such as large changes in worker productivity or consumer requests. Finally, you consult the new list of indicative prices adjusted according to relative excess demands and supplies in first round proposals. Then you make any changes you wish before entering your second proposal.

Once everyone does the same, all these new proposals are summed and the new information is made available for the third round of planning. So far, so good: in the first two rounds, no rules that limit changes. But not necessarily rapid convergence, either.

Now, however, in the third round, there would be a change. We would no longer move our proposals in any direction by any amount. Now, in an effort to facilitate convergence without introducing biases, there are limits on how much consumers can increase or decrease their demand for goods. While the specific limits that best facilitate convergence would probably differ for different goods, and settling the limits may well be something best left to the discretion of industry IFBs who develop a "feel" for what works best in their industry, at this point consumers would be prohibited from decreasing demand for a good in excess demand by (say) more than 50 percent of the average per capita excess demand, while they would be prohibited from increasing demand for a good in excess demand by more than (say) 25 percent of the average per capita excess demand. And likewise, consumers would also be prohibited from increasing their demand for a good in excess supply by more than 50 percent of the average per capita excess supply and from decreasing demand for such a good by more than 25 percent of the average per capita excess supply. Similarly, producers would have a comparable rule, to be initially applied, however, only in the fourth iteration so that most reallocation of labor could already be settled, where each factory would be limited to the same range of

*"Having markets, we also have banks which in turn have competing branches in virtually every community utilizing enough buildings to house a comparable participatory economy's nonworkplace, nonconsumption housed facilitation boards."*

Freedom only for the supporters of the government, only for the members of the party—however numerous they may be—is no freedom as all. Freedom is always and exclusively freedom for the one who thinks differently. Not because of any fanatical concept of justice but because all that is instructive, wholesome, and purifying in political freedom depends on this essential characteristic, and its effectiveness vanishes when freedom becomes a special privilege.
—Rosa Luxemburg
in Cohn Bendit, *Obsolete Communism*

movement, but of their factory's *proportionate share* of the gap between supply and demand. In other words, actors' changes are limited, assuming this rule is employed, more if they want to change in the direction that takes the status of a good away from equilibrium, and less if they want to change in the direction that moves the status of the good toward equilibrium. The rule's purpose is to guarantee that the maximum possible divergence from equilibrium diminishes with each iteration. The limit pressures actors not to be frivolous about early proposals lest they place themselves too far from where they will want to end up to be able to get there under the limitations. The different limit for the two types of movement insures that if goods move from excess demand to excess supply or vice versa, they will most likely do so in ways that leave the gap between supply and demand diminished. Whether it is better to choose limits of 75 percent and 40 percent or 30 percent and 10 percent instead of 50 percent and 25 percent will depend on the iteration, the good, and perhaps other features of the economy as well. But the point is that some limits, with equilibrating changes less restricted than disequilibrating changes, will increase the expected speed of convergence. These types of limits, therefore, are examples of potentially useful facilitation rules for participatory planning.

In the fourth round of planning, full councils make proposals instead of individuals. Consumers meet in their neighborhood councils and workers in their workplace councils to decide councilwide proposals. This is when individuals must convince neighbors and workmates that above average consumption requests and below average work proposals are warranted. And if cases are not deemed compelling, local pressure, including the possibility of a council rejecting a proposal, is applied to individuals to make adjustments. In workplaces, in particular, the need for coordination causes debate to settle on shared views about overall workload and intensity.

Nothing about this approach compels actors to change proposals at all or pushes consumers to consume goods in the same proportions or workers to produce goods with the same techniques. On the other hand, there is pressure on workplaces to propose at least average amounts of productive labor and on consumer councils to limit consumption to roughly average per capita value and on all actors to assess their needs and capacities carefully right from the outset of the process.

*"Nothing about this approach compels actors to change proposals at all or pushes consumers to consume goods in the same proportions or workers to produce goods with the same techniques."*

Indeed, at this stage, workplaces that persist in proposals with lower social benefit to cost ratios than their industry's must petition their industry to be allowed to persist. Similarly, neighborhood consumer councils ordering above-average per capita consumption bundles would have to petition higher-level councils for permission not to lower their demands. This process would curtail inequitable proposals but would be subject to sensible discretion. We would expect many petitions to be granted because there are frequently extenuating circumstances.

Getting back to the unadorned process, if I really like nuts and have a way above-average request for them, I do not need to lower my request for nuts simply because nuts are in excess demand. I may decide my large request for nuts is more than justified given my low demand for fruit. Or, especially if it's an early round of planning, I may think that in future rounds the supply of nuts needs to go up and will. Ultimately there will be pressure on consumption councils to reduce nuts' demand and on production councils to increase nuts' supply if the status of "nuts" doesn't improve. For one thing, the indicative price of nuts will keep rising as long as nuts are in excess demand. And for another, if the gap is disruptive, IFBs may begin making suggestions. In the end, I may hold to my above-average demand for nuts while someone with a below-average demand for nuts lowers his or her demand even further in face of a rising indicative price. This simply means I have a strong preference for nuts compared to others. It is not unfair because I will have to consume less of other goods and those who lowered their demands for nuts will be able to consume more of other goods.

The fifth round (or a later one, if that makes more sense) involves a new twist that greatly accelerates planning. Again we meet in councils to adapt our proposals in accord with changing information about averages, totals, prices, and so on. But this time the IFBs extrapolate from the experience of the previous four rounds to

One might argue that facilitation boards will require many buildings spread throughout the society. Consider that Century 21 has 7,005 franchises, Electronic Realty Associates 2,596, and H&R Block 3,886 and that all of these are already tightly networked and together constitute only a small percentage of the buildings that are available for transfer without any new construction at all and with a reduction in staffing requirements. If that isn't enough to make the point, consider that we currently have 6,165 McDonald's, 5,782 Kentucky Fried Chicken, 5,122 Dairy Queen, 3,500 Subway Sandwiches, 3,300 Baskin Robbins, and 2,597 Wendy's chains. If we replaced all these, and many many more, with 15,000 *all purpose* establishments the remaining 10,000 to 15,000 units would all be available.

provide their best estimates of (say) five feasible plans that could plausibly be the final outcome of the iteration process. What distinguishes their five options might be different ratios of consumption to investment goods, and/or different proportions of public to private goods, and slightly different amounts of total product/work expended. All actors then vote, as units, for one of these five feasible plans. Votes are tallied and the options with the two lowest totals are eliminated. Subsequent votes are held until a single option remains, establishing *a total product* and thus an average per capita work and consumption projection for the whole economy, as well as proportions for consumption, investment, public, and private goods. Once this feasible "macro" plan is settled, further iterations refine only the individual unit assignments. The percentage change permitted in proposals is also reduced for subsequent planning to reduce the possibility of over adjustments that prolong the process.

Finally, the IFBs propose a comprehensive plan within a small margin of each unit's previous proposals. In the final round, each council receives this plan and votes whether to accept it. If alterations are still desired, they must be accommodated within federations—for example, if a neighborhood wants more of something, another neighborhood in the ward must take less—or changes must be negotiated directly with producers who must agree to fulfill additional requests out of slack even though doing so may mean that they will have to work more later. These communications within and between relevant industry and consumer units go on until a plan for all units and individuals is accepted.

The above discussion outlines the contours of one possible system of rules for participatory planning and is intended only as an example. In different societies, and even in the same society at different times, rules will correspond to contemporary tastes and circumstances. Actors themselves will set the procedures. If a society's ability to transfer resources from one productive use to another were effectively perfect, there might be no such rules at all since in that case just indicative prices and the need to have one's overall proposal be equitable along with attention to qualitative details would be sufficient to engender a rapid convergence of supply and demand. On the other hand, in less developed economies less technically able to quickly accommodate changing preferences or in which some goods might be given artificially low prices to insure their availability for social reasons, iteration rules more or less like those we have described might prove important to facilitate convergence.

## Allocation Alternatives

So what do we now have? Is the feasible plan that a participatory economy will converge to efficient and equitable? Or will all the bargaining yield an outcome no better than those that result from central planning or markets?

Our answer to these questions should be obvious from previous comments. The equality, solidarity, diversity, and democracy that participatory planning promotes in place of the exploitation, class division, conformity, and hierarchy that characterize capitalist *and* coordinator economies more than justify a change to the new system. The fact that participatory planning will also be more efficient than markets or central planning clinches the case. [We refer interested readers to chapter 5 of this book's companion volume, *The Political Economy of Participatory Economics* (Princeton 1991), for a rigorous demonstration that this is, indeed, so.] Only fear that participatory planning might involve an intolerable bureaucracy remains a pressing concern, so, to allay this fear, we now present a brief comparison between the institutional and time requirements of our model and nonparticipatory alternatives.

Of course, the main allocation institution in any capitalist society is the market which doesn't directly involve employees of any sort since it is "only" a set of relations and rules applying to the interfaces between economic actors and institutions. However, the market does impose a whole host of implications calling forth particular competitive and accounting behaviors in all institutions. Moreover the market imposes a need for many institutions that would not otherwise exist whether in the presence of private property or not.

For example, having markets, we also have banks which have branches in virtually every community utilizing enough buildings to house most if not all of a participatory economy's production and

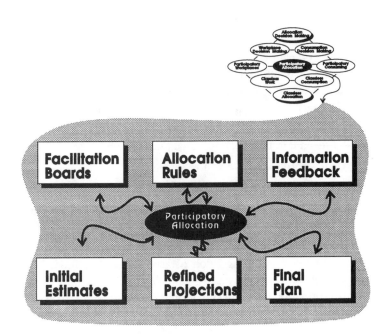

There are currently in the U.S. just under 300,000 finance and insurance establishments, including banks, credit agencies, commodity brokers, insurance carriers, and just over 200,000 real estate offices. Together these employ nearly 6.4 million people. To get a feeling for what the transfer of all this to more socially useful purposes would allow in terms of units per population and region, consider that in the U.S. there are only 187,430 food stores, 362,895 eating and drinking places, and 201,631 automotive service stores and service stations, altogether employing 10.5 million people. These numbers indicate the relative size of market paraphernalia.

consumption facilitation boards. With markets we also have insurance companies with tens of thousands of employees, likely more employees than we would need in our updating facilitation boards. And with markets we have stock exchanges, credit card companies, and brokerage firms as well as bloated police forces and private security agencies far beyond what security and oversight would require in a participatory system. We have advertising agencies, auditing agencies, and, of course, the Internal Revenue Service as well as state, county, and municipal tax bureaus, with few similar needs in participatory economics. And, of course, we also have product redundancy and advertising expenditures galore.

Will facilitation boards and job complexes within plants and consumer units use all the material and human resources liberated when the institutional paraphernalia of markets disappear? We seriously doubt that the institutional apparatus of participatory planning compares unfavorably with the institutional apparatus of markets or central planning.

We have now presented a description of the basic structure of participatory economics. To get more of a feel for how the system will actually work, in the following three chapters we present descriptions of the behavior of hypothetical actors developing plans in different contexts. As a conclusion for this chapter, however, we would like to present a final discussion that took place between our usual protagonists shortly after PE described participatory planning, much as you have just read.

## Is This for Real?

CENT: You claim central planning subverts participatory aims, but your vision would only yield chaos. Your model is so cumbersome that any sensible person would prefer mine or Mark's. You don't really mean for participatory economics to be other than a provocation, do you?

PE: I mean it to be a superior allocation system.

CAP: It's hard to believe you're serious.

PE: What makes you think participatory economics won't work?

MARK: Who will agree to so many meetings? People won't attend, and if you force them to, they'll be so put out they'll either muck things up or slit their wrists in frustration.

CAP: I agree. Assuming I don't starve waiting for food, I would approach your economy as a gigantic game I would play by giving misinformation, couching my proposals to elicit desired responses, and lying about my motives to win excessive requests. Eventually I wouldn't do anything I didn't want to whether I had promised to or not. Your system's a joke.

CENT: That's right. Even with central planners watching for people like Cap, such behavior is hard to prevent. You don't even worry about these problems.

PE: The joke is that many people behave as you've just described in your economies, but not even you would behave that way in my economy. Of course all manner of obnoxious dealings occur in capitalist and coordinator economies. What Cap, Cent, and you too, Mark, expect participatory actors to do is only a transplanted version of how workers and consumers operate in your economies: everyone playing every opportunity for all its worth, trying to push themselves ahead regardless of the impact on others. But other than spite, what leads you to predict such problems in participatory economies? In a participatory economy one can't cheat to get rich or even to escape work, except maybe by faking illness. Remember, it's your neighbors and workmates you'd have to fool. Not a boss on a cruise in the Caribbean or a planner 3,000 miles away.

Given that each person winds up with a roughly average set of burdens and benefits, the real issue is having a say in what that average will be, deciding whether to borrow or loan, and determining the particular components of one's own work and consumption. Misrepresentation is self-defeating.

MARK: There is something to what you say—in fact, examining it without prejudice, all you've done is replace markets with a primative barter system. And in some respects you've come closer to the "ideal" sought in free market exchange than free marketeers because you've eliminated monopoly, monopsony, cartels, and various technical problems associated with markets…

PE: …More important, the new system eliminates the antisocial bias of markets…

MARK: …But we're not talking about establishing a system to work on some tiny island or for a group of friends going on a two-month outing. It doesn't mean much that you've overcome difficult problems present in realistic models by proposing an alternative only applicable to tiny economies where everyone can know everything. What about allocating goods and services for an economy with millions of actors and hundreds of thousands of products? What is the information burden in *that* context? Do you seriously believe we are all going to carefully choose among all available product options?

PE: Exactly. If we group products so that similar items are considered under one label—alcoholic beverages, beef, shirts (dress, heavy, and light), cars (large and small), trips (by time and distance), records, books—and if we eliminate all products that have little use value, and if goods aren't made to wear out so we don't replace everything so often; is there really too much to assess? Do you realize that right now, in our society, four or five credit companies have files on upward of 50 million people and use those files actively? Hard as it may be to believe, moving and managing

…It is clear that someone (some institution) has to tell the producer about what the users require. If that 'someone' is not the impersonal market mechanism it can only be a hierarchical superior. There are horizontal links (market), there are vertical links (hierarchy). What other dimension is there? Of course, the producers are also consumers, and vice versa, but an inescapable division of labor and of function imply that this is so only at the top of an all-inclusive hierarchical pyramid.

—Alec Nove
*The Economics of Feasible Socialism*

It is no longer enough to point out what we don't like, we have to work out 'what sort of society we do want'…

—Sheila Rowbotham
*Dreams and Dilemmas*

The bureaucratic centralist form of planning, in which what those at the top receive from below is principally only passive factual information and 'questions,' while what they hand down are actual imperatives, stamps the mechanism by which tasks are allotted to individuals. It is a point of principle that people do not have to seek tasks for themselves, recognize and deal with problems, but they are rather assigned to tasks as duties.

—Rudolph Bahro

How can one show that resources used for library A should not go to library B, or for that matter to improve a science laboratory or the diet of children in kindergartens in Kampuchea? Or that the provision of a better telescope for an observatory is more or less important than building a new bridge, growing more carrots, investing in a new cement works, or increasing the size of coffee plantations?
—Alec Nove
*The Economics of Feasible Socialism*

When the workers are society they will regulate their labour, so that the supply and demand shall be genuine, not gambling; the two will then be commensurate, for it is the same society which demands that also supplies; there will be no more artificial famines then, no more poverty amidst overproduction, amidst too great a stock of the very things which should supply poverty and turn it into well being. In short there will be no waste and therefore no tyranny.
—William Morris
*How We Live and How We Might Live*

information, summarizing it, averaging it, and otherwise shaping it into useful formats that people can relate to won't be a big deal.

And regarding assessing purchases in advance, actually much of what is produced in modern economies is bought by companies and other institutions that already pass judgment on alternative possibilities well in advance, as, for example, when General Motors estimates car production and puts in orders for rubber, steel, etc. As far as time and energy is concerned, this not only can be done, it is done, though, particularly in market economies, often using the wrong data. I ought to also mention that as a bonus there will be no question of different brand names since whole industries will be internally coordinated to use the best available techniques and create a diversity of products of the highest quality. Instead of competition breeding innovation, special workplaces and teams in each workplace will have this responsibility.

CENT: But who can sit down and list everything he or she wants for a whole year? And who would want to?

PE: You will sit at a computer console and go over a list of your consumption for last year and consider expected changes in society's total product and indicative prices for this year. In addition, you'll access some information about what is entailed in making products, and what their advantages and disadvantages may be. You'll punch out a personal consumption plan, alter it some, and then make it your first proposal. And yes, you will be able to go to showrooms to see new products and to try out ones you are unfamiliar with, choosing models with different refinements, even though you don't bother with such details at the planning stage.

CAP: He's raving…

PE: Nonsense. Shopping around might take time, but that's true now, too. Settling on a first proposal after shopping around might take as little as a few sessions of a few hours each or, in any event, less than thirty hours spread over the course of three weeks. For most people it won't take as long as filling out income tax forms now, or as the time spent dealing now with loans and bills over a few months, none of which delightful pastimes will exist in participatory economies.

No more driving to 3 stores looking for bargains. No more clipping coupons and licking green stamps. And Cent, no more standing in lines that you have not figured out how to get rid of in 70 years of trying. Consider how much time people spend shopping now—not just pleasantly browsing, but trying to find bargains, getting food each week in crowded supermarkets, or waiting on line for service. Think about a whole year's worth of that and then think about the time it would take to work on your participatory proposal and how much more interesting the latter project would be.

Yes, you would also have to update your proposal during iterations, 10 hours max, each time. Certainly some of the council meetings where you consume or work would be lengthy and exasperating. But for consumption planning, in any case, you can not attend or leave whenever you choose. Once a plan was set, subsequent shopping would be infrequent and subsequent workplace decision making would be without the hassles of catering to bosses. Much of what we seek to consume will be delivered to council outlets or even communities. Imagine the time *that* will save.

MARK: But what we want each week will continually change. Even if your slack and update techniques allow plans to accommodate the whole population, regarding weekly deliveries I certainly won't be able to decide in advance what I want every week unless I know when I'm going to have guests, when I'm going to eat out, and so on, a whole year in advance. Nobody knows that.

PE: That's true, so in our society we will put in orders for food deliveries on a monthly or weekly basis, whatever makes sense. And even though your order may fluctuate each week, it is averaged with the orders of everyone else in your neighborhood, so shippers are less likely to be surprised by bulk orders. The whole idea of averages allowing localized fluctuations with minimal inconvenience to producers works rather similarly in market and centrally planned economies.

For example, imagine that in a market economy everyone unpredictably decides they want twice as much milk, or shoes, or whatever. They would encounter delays probably worse than in participatory economies because the participatory model has much better communicative facilities. But if I were to offer this as a weakness of markets, Mark and Cap would just laugh it off. These things don't happen any more than other freak events of low probability. So why bring them up only when criticizing participatory planning? It wastes time and obscures truth. We would only have a problem if we had no means for updating plans in light of changed circumstances, tastes, etc. But we do have such means in the participatory system.

MARK: What about resources? How can your system properly value resources?

PE: Participatory allocation is designed to generate more accurate estimates of social costs and benefits than any other economy ever has—even though I probably attach less weight to efficiency than participation, equity, solidarity, etc., than any of you. Not only are our "indicative" prices the product of a social iterative process—which your Austrian school of supporters, Cap, correctly points out is the only basis for arriving at reasonable estimates—but the social process is equitable due to job complex balancing and fair incomes and is also arranged by the use of councils at many levels to reflect the subtle mixture of private and social interests at stake in human economies. That's one reason indicative prices will more accurately estimate true social costs and benefits then Cap's or Mark's or Cent's prices. The other reason is that we provide participants in

Power always acts destructively, for its possessors are ever striving to lace all phenomena of social life into a corset of their laws to give them a definite shape. Its mental expression is dead dogma; its physical manifestation of life, brute force. This lack of intelligence in its endeavors leaves its imprint likewise on the persons of its representatives, gradually making them inferior and brutal, even though they were originally excellently endowed. Nothing dulls the mind and the soul of man as does the eternal monotony of routine, and power is essentially routine.

—Rudolf Rocker
*Nationalism and Culture*

People's lives are in turmoil. There is a sense of crisis for men as well as for women, and for children too. Do we have an idea or even a glimmering about how people can and should live, not as victims as in the past for women, nor as atoms just whirling around on their own trajectories, but as members of a human community and as moral agents in that community?

—Barbara Ehrenreich
*DSA pamphlet*

One may argue, while still remaining within the logic of the system, about who should tell people where they can build houses—the ministry, the planning office, or the municipality—but no one can question that *somebody has to tell them* where they can build without betraying the whole class ethos.
—George Konrad and Ivan Szelenyi
*The Intellectuals on the Road to Class Power*

There is…only a single categorical imperative and it is this: Act only on that maxim through which you can at the same time will that it should become a universal law.
—Immanuel Kant
*The Metaphysic of Morals*

the social process of price estimation with qualitative data that improves human abilities to act knowledgeably. If that's not enough to shut you hypocrites up on the issue of rational prices, nothing ever will be.

CAP: You're good at knocking us around, but why won't the members of your boards cheat? It seems that every time anything happens the iteration facilitation boards are involved, and then during the year it seems the production and consumption updating facilitation boards become important. I'd like to have a cushy spot on one of those.

PE: Just how would you take advantage? Suppose you and a bunch of your cronies are all on a high-level IFB or UFB. Presumably, there are two approaches to cheating. You could enrich yourself by biasing outcomes in favor of someone willing to pay you off or you could simply bias outcomes in your own favor directly. The latter possibility could be trivially undone by guaranteeing that individuals don't handle data bearing on their own economic activities. But I think this is actually overkill since facilitation boards merely manipulate data and project hypothetical outcomes, which then serve as further data that producers and consumers use however they like. Facilitators do not decide anything. Anyhow, all their calculations and projections can be checked.

But let's assume a worst-case scenario. It's early in a planning process, the stage of determining collective consumption for a county, and an issue on the agenda is whether to construct a high-quality skating rink for county use. A group of citizens who are avid skaters, one of whom has a son who is a potential Olympian, are eager for the rink to be voted up. Others are opposed, but naturally the whole thing will hinge to a great extent on the amount of work required for the project. In such a situation, calculations can be very important. And duplication of efforts and oversight might be uneconomical, unlike in the case of national accounting. This is the participatory cheat's best chance.

So let's say you are on the relevant local board and you want to make a killing. You are clever and sure you can trick everybody into a report that understates the costs of the rink by 20 percent, more than enough to ensure that it will be passed. How you would do this, given that costs would have to be determined via inquiries to producers about their services and none of them would have any interest in lying is beyond me, but let's say you could pull it off.

So you meet with John, whose son is the potential Olympian and a few other skating fanatics and offer to sell your support for a price. Now what? They can't offer money because they don't have any. They only have their own personal "credit card" computers that keep track of their consumption and allow easy accounting for purposes of oversight and analysis by the UFBs. They could offer personal services or they might offer to submit consumption requests that favor items you like and make presents of those items to you, but that's about it. The absence of large income and wealth differentials and the non-existence of exchangeable money would make bribery rather difficult. Of course it isn't ruled out. They could also approach you rather than you them, and threaten you if you don't help them out. Are we reduced to debating this type of nonsense?

CAP: What a godawful lot of bureaucracy all that must add up to...

PE: Any comparison of the various facilitation boards I have described, many of which only operate part time, with the infinite paraphernalia of today's accountants, finance departments, insurance companies, stock exchanges, banks, lending agencies, and state bureaucracies of countless types, not to mention excessive advertising...

CAP: Why shouldn't I and my work mates exaggerate the human costs of work we do to win approval for a proposal to work fewer hours?

PE: But wouldn't similar companies' averages reveal your lie?

CAP: Let's say there are very few and we're all in it together. We meet in our industry council—an ideal setting for turning self-pity into plotting. Indeed, why wouldn't everyone do it?

PE: Take it further. My work mates and I can claim we can't produce much, and wait for more employees to be approved. But it's a lie, so we all loaf when the new employees show up. Alternatively, as you say, we can work hard and produce at a reasonable pace, but claim there are real hardships involved that make the work very burdensome so we should have to work fewer hours. Both these flummeries are possible. But they stand a reasonable chance of being detected. First, production units are held accountable for the resources they use—including the human resources they are assigned. It won't do to pretend that workers trained as electrical engineers can't accomplish much unless more are sent since every unit is effectively charged the value of electrical engineers *elsewhere*. If they aren't able to produce much of value in one workplace, they will end up being assigned elsewhere since the social benefit to social cost ratio of the unit will prove unacceptable.

Second, lying about work conditions will be revealed by workers voting with their feet. If all workers in the publishing industry conspire to perpetrate an official lie that publishing work is tough, even if they put it over on the planning system, unofficial word will leak out that things are cushy in publishing and the excess of applicants to openings will tip off job complex balancing committees that something is amiss.

In any case, though the system does have guards against these types of behavior due to its equity and solidarity inducing priorities, I suspect there won't be any generalized goofing off of the type you describe, only isolated instances. And I suspect the sum total of those isolated instances will come to a very small fraction of the interminable screwing around and active avoidance of getting things done that exists in workplaces where workers are lorded over

Society is no comfort to one not sociable.

—Shakespeare
*Cymbeline*

...all authority is quite degrading. It degrades those who exercise it, and degrades those over whom it is exercised....When it is used with a certain amount of kindness, and accompanied by prizes and rewards, it is dreadfully demoralizing. People, in that case, are less conscious of the horrible pressure that is being put on them, and so go through their lives in a sort of coarse comfort, like petted animals, without ever realizing that they are probably thinking other people's thoughts, living by other people's standards, wearing practically what one may call other people's secondhand clothes, and never being themselves for a single moment. "He who would be free," says a fine thinker, "must not conform." And authority, by bribing people to conform, produces a very gross kind of overfed barbarism amongst us.

—Oscar Wilde
*The Soul of Man under Socialism*

Equal wealth and equal opportunities of culture...have simply made us all members of one class.
—Edward Bellamy
*Looking Backward*

and exploited by owners and managers and rightfully rebel against it. But then I have a much more complimentary view of human nature and of what people will be like in desirable, comfortable surroundings than you do. However, if you should prove closer to the mark, it would not be particularly difficult to create workplaces whose purpose was to examine other workplaces and assess jobs to make sure reports are accurate.

MARK: And if those workers cheat, too?

PE: Of course, if you assume as a starting point that given the chance everyone would rather take advantage of their neighbor than share with them in an equal, fulfilling social effort, then any participatory proposal can be ridiculed. But think about how little out-and-out dishonesty there is even in societies that debase people, offer every opportunity to cheat, and often celebrate cheating. After all, most of us don't even jump subway turnstiles or ignore parking meters even when we know we can get away with it, or—even more indicative—fail to leave tips for waiters and waitresses at restaurants we will never return to.

People can't be motivated to work by the pleasure of contributing to the community and of doing a good job in a creative way when they have no control over their workplaces, know little about where their products go, don't determine the character of their output, and earn pitiful incomes. But by reversing all these relations we can bring people's sociability to the fore.

CENT: It's all well and good to discuss the process abstractly. We used to talk about central planning like that and it seemed like it would work flawlessly as well. But in practice there are so many unforseen details and complexities. It seems to me your system is ill-equipped to handle those, to bend, to function efficiently...

PE: Perhaps some detailed descriptions will help. However, in thinking abstractly, as you say, about participatory planning, markets, and central planning, it seems to me that participatory planning is the most flexible and least internally inconsistent of the bunch. After all, markets are horrible at dealing with externalities, public goods, and ecological issues and thereby create grave contradictions for themselves even as they promote antisocial behavior by elevating competition and rewarding corruption. Similarly, central planning relies on units that are alienated and hierarchically organized and on actors most likely providing unreliable data and carrying out orders with something less than zeal.

But participatory planning calls forth the skills and attitudes people must have if the system is to yield optimal outcomes. It is internally consistent and generates calculations that account for externalities, public goods, and the overall qualitative development of the economy. Nonetheless, I can certainly understand your hesitance. After all, I know all we've done is talk abstractly. So let's see what the details of a planning process might look like.

# 7

# Workplace Decision Making

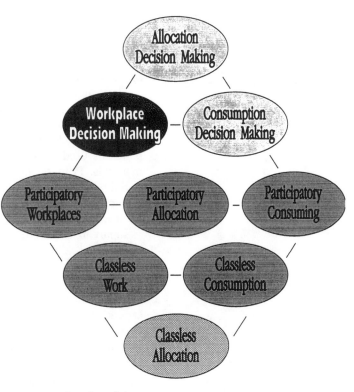

*Necessity is the argument of tyrants. It is the creed of slaves.*
—William Pitt Jr.

**A**ssume our workplaces, consumer units, and allocation system have all been transformed, years of successful economic operations have been pleasurably experienced, and people are old hands at participatory economic planning—whatever other ills and idiosyncrasies they may have. Here's how they might make yearly production plans in the context of reasonable choices by other actors throughout the economy.

## Planning at Northstart

**P**articipatory planning occurs as each unit makes, debates, and amends its own proposals and evaluates the proposals of others. What does this process look like at Northstart publishing house?

### Last Year at Northstart

When workers begin their yearly planning, first they review the prior year's plan and particularly any changes from what they initially proposed. We remember that work always uses inputs including social relations in the workplace, workers with specific skills and social characteristics, and resources, equipment, and intermediate goods produced at other workplaces. Work also generates outputs including altered social relations, personalities, and skills of workers as well as products others will use. Workers' plans thus always include three lists: material and social/personal inputs; work relations, policies, motivations and logic; and material and personal/social outputs.

There is but one unconditional commandment, which is that we should seek incessantly, with fear and trembling, so to vote and to act as to bring about the very largest total of good which we can see.
—William James
*The Moral Philosopher and the Moral Life*

Then, regarding the composition of these lists, more outputs require more inputs, certain choices of work relations require more inputs for given outputs, and a different mix of inputs with a fixed set of work relations may yield different outputs.

Northstart's primary outputs are computer records of books, communication of books to readers, modified relationships with readers, and changes in worker attributes and plant social relations. Secondary products include a small number of bound books, waste materials, used equipment, and leftover supplies of paper and other materials. Primary inputs are workers' skills and efforts, plant social relations; utilities such as gas, water, electricity, and communication, a building, old equipment, new equipment, paper, and diverse supplies like light bulbs and pencils.

Inputs are broken roughly into two major categories: investment goods which allow alteration of the scale or methods of production, and production goods which allow operations at a chosen scale with determined social relations. The main "work relations choices" determine how work will be organized, how many hours will be expended each day, and what technologies will be employed. Any change of work relations will likely require some changes in inputs and outputs, and vice versa.

One way to envision these relations would be to graph outputs for varying combinations of inputs for each possible choice of technology and work relations. A more practical tool for local analysis would be simple programs showing inputs required per outputs preferred for possible work relations. These programs would make possible an easy estimation of workplace plans for each possible work-relation decision by helping workers highlight how choices affect productive possibilities.

On the following page we display a computer screen view of such a program. Any Northstart worker can call it up on a computer, enter choices for technology and social relations, and see what inputs would yield a given list of outputs, or what outputs a given list of inputs could generate. The technology required to create such programs already exists. To use them one needs only have a good understanding of workplace relations. No sophisticated programming knowledge is required. The assumption that a simple program can incorporate alternative choices of social relations is not so reductionist as it may at first seem to some readers. We imply only that the program, properly prepared by iteration workers, can quickly show the best estimates of the material implications of alternative options. It could even list the qualitative features that differ from option to option, as these were determined by workers themselves and entered in the program by facilitation workers prior to the planning period. Of course, when people finally vote on options, the spreadsheet only facilitates manipulating information. Workers' feelings about what they envision to be the implications of the different choices guide the decisions they make.

Next, a brief plant meeting informs everyone of national IFB projections of trends for the coming year including initial projections for overall growth, incomes, and indicative prices, as well as

## Northstart Planning Program -- Screen One

| WorkPlace Options | Option 1 | Option 2 | Option 3 | Option 4 |
|---|---|---|---|---|
| Technology (Click Box): | ▮ | X | ▮ | ▮ |
| Social Relations (Click Box): | ▮ | ▮ | X | ▮ |
| Employees (Enter #): | 100% ▮ | | | |

| Inputs | | | Outputs | |
|---|---|---|---|---|
| Paper: | 107% | ? | Titles Published: | 110% ▮ |
| Office Supplies: | 105% | ? | Books Fulfilled: | 130% ▮ |
| Utilities: | 103% | ? | Work Effects | ▨ |
| Bldg Maint. and Depreciation: | 102% | ? | Consumer Effects | ▨ |
| Equipment Depreciation: | 101% | ? | | |
| Equipment Investment: | $20,000 | ? | | |
| Ave. Hrs Labor Per Worker: | 22 | ? | | |

> Enter data as amounts or as a % of last year or enter a ? for the program to calculate the variable based on other choices. Click on label Inputs or Outputs to initiate recalculation..

> Click any box for help, Double click any box for additional qualitative information or for worksheets to allow more detailed data entry.

### Work Load Implications

| | | | |
|---|---|---|---|
| Proj Societal Ave Hours Labor: | 33 | Work Hour Range at Northstart: | 20 to 28 |
| Northstart Job Complex Ranking: | 80% | Offsetting Work Hour Range Elsewhere: | 5 to 13 |

> The worker using this worksheet first chose technology option 2 and social relations option 3 (after double clicking the relevant boxes for more detailed descriptions) and then decided to test the case where employee level would be the same as last year. She entered ? for all inputs and chose a preferred output level after double clicking on the relevant boxes to check qualitative information regarding effects of work and output on workers and consumers as well as details about titles to be published and audience to be reached. She then double clicked on the word inputs and the program calculated inputs and work load implications for her preferred outputs. She later varied choices to refine her plan preferences.

industry IFB projections including qualitative summaries of publishing's impact on readers last year, explanations of changes expected this year, and plant IFB proposals for changes in plant organization, technologies, or policies, including detailed descriptions of human and social implications of projected changes in material inputs and outputs.

We should note that for purposes of simplifying discussion, here we ignore long-term investment planning which we treat in chapter 9. So, assuming long-term investment decisions have already been settled, in assessing last year's data and this year's projections workers begin weighing their own desires and prepare to register the social relations, technology, and input and output levels they prefer for Northstart. The first and second round of plant decision making require workers to choose individually with no requirement that their selections be mutually compatible.

### Northstart Innovations

Before following Northstart planning, however, we should note one very important aspect of settling on plant organization and technology. Each worker decides what alterations in plant operations she or he wants to request. To achieve these changes she or he registers preferences for investments. The ensuing changes might, for example, diminish the output-to-input ratio to improve quality of work life, or might change how much work she or he has to do given the demand for books. Whatever changes Northstart workers finally decide they want, they have to get an okay from the system as a whole, assuming they need additional inputs.

The important thing to note is that if Northstart workers request and receive significant workplace changes that dramatically improve quality of worklife at Northstart, this benefit will eventually be shared with other workers. How much work anyone does away from his or her main workplace depends on the quality of work differentials between that main workplace and society's average. Thus, when innovations significantly diminish the burdensomeness of work at one plant, the result, after job balancing committees have time to assess the change, is that each employee spends fewer hours there and more hours elsewhere. Innovations that make Northstart work relatively more pleasurable will change the time Northstart workers work there and elsewhere. So because of the principle that all workers enjoy comparable overall job responsibilities, gains accruing from Northstart investments manifest themselves in slightly improved conditions *for all workers* rather than in dramatically improved conditions only for Northstart employees. Therefore, workers have little reason to urge innovations in their own plants at the expense of innovations that could be enacted elsewhere with a more dramatic effect on quality of worklife. In short, after appropriate adjustments in work scheduling I would benefit more from greater improvements elsewhere than from improvements with less impact where I spend most of my time.

Traditional economists will argue that this will diminish workers' incentives to improve the quality of worklife, since workers will not be able to monopolize the gains they engineer. But this view conveniently ignores that in competitive models of capitalism technological gains are assumed to spread instantaneously to all producers in an industry. If this were not assumed, in these models it could not be claimed that they yield efficient results. But when it is assumed, incentives to innovate diminish since benefits spread first to other firms in the industry, and later through lower costs of production and lower price for the industry's output, to all producers and consumers. Of course, in real capitalism, as opposed to economists' models of it, improvements do not spread and the benefits of innovation accrue almost exclusively to a small number of owners—certainly not to workers—and there are consequent inefficiencies. In any case, since in an equitable economy technological improvements must rebound to *everyone's* benefit, we consider it a virtue that in a participatory economy innovations in thousands of plants change the *overall societal average work load and work quality norms* and that those changes in turn rebound equally to *everyone's* benefit.

So what does this reduce to in practice? If Larry works at Northstart and a proposal for a technological change there and throughout publishing would improve the average job complex for society by one hundredth of a percent, while a proposal for the steel industry (requiring the same investment expenditure) would improve the average by two hundredths of a percent, Larry will eventually benefit more from the steel innovation than from the publishing change. Likewise, Northstart workers have a greater long-term interest in an innovation in coal mining that greatly improves that industry's quality of work than in an innovation in publishing that would require an equivalent investment but improve the quality of publishing work to a lesser degree.

Larry's tastes, whether slight or great, are therefore summed with those of all other publishing workers and embodied in the evaluation of possible publishing industry alterations *before any comparison with other industry proposals* occurs. If Larry's views differ dramatically from the collective result, Larry will not necessarily like the final outcome. But the choice will reflect a fair balance of the tastes of *all* workers in both industries. Larry should vote as he likes, and if he does so, and all other workers do so as well, the collective implications noted earlier will apply.

It follows that the war of each against all for who will benefit from innovations gives way to a community of shared interests. Competition is replaced by cooperation. Shortening work hours anywhere eventually benefits all. Improving work life anywhere eventually benefits all. An equitable economy requires all this, but to increase individual incentives job balancing committees could calibrate the speed of adjustments to provide temporary "material incentives" to innovators. Or, alternatively, teams could be assigned whose job was to develop potential innovations. This would be their "output" by which their social usefulness would be judged. The equity implications of this way to stimulate innovation, essentially assigning more resources to innovation and holding those who use them socially accountable, has more desirable human repercussions in our view. In any event, in deciding on innovations that have been well characterized, each actor chooses between proposals however they wish, but everyone has an incentive in a participatory economy to choose what is best for the whole economy because that is what is best for all actors. Ironically, the claim made propagandistically for markets—that pursuit of individual interests coincides with the social interest—actually holds for participatory planning. Pursuit of self-fulfillment under equitable arrangements and in a socially conscious way really does yield socially optimal outcomes.

Moreover, participatory economics' solidarity-promoting dynamic does not derive from some presumed biological transformation of our genetic characteristics, but from the concrete implications of actual social relationships. Desirable results promoting solidarity, variety, and collective self-management are not assumed because we postulate a suddenly beatific human nature, but because the structure and incentives of the participatory planning process promote these goals. Beside linking individual and collective well being, the system promotes participation, empathy, sociability, and the qualitative side of life that has been under attack since the dawn of capitalism over 300 years ago!

My own hopes and intuitions are that self-fulfilling and creative work is a fundamental human need, and that the pleasures of a challenge met, work well done, the exercise of skill and craftsmanship, are real and significant, and are an essential part of a full and meaningful life. The same is true of the opportunity to understand and enjoy the achievements of others, which often go beyond what we ourselves can do, and to work constructively in cooperation with others.

—Noam Chomsky
*Language and Politics*

*"Shortening work hours anywhere eventually benefits all. Improving work life anywhere eventually benefits all."*

### The First Planning Iteration: Nancy's Initial Proposal

Nancy has worked at Northstart for eight years and is predominantly concerned with science books and promotion. In preparing her initial proposal for Northstart's new year she considers three proposals for reorganization that workers who investigate innovations have proposed. While recognizing that Northstart already has an above average work complex, Nancy believes plan three would greatly improve work quality by freeing energies from distracting tasks with modest investment. She estimates that while not as valuable as some proposed transformations in heavy industries she has heard about, proposal three would be worthwhile compared to most innovations under consideration.

Indeed, the idea of a projected lower bound that proposed investment projects should attain in increased output or improved work conditions per investment required is part of the information the national production facilitation board would provide. Wherever workers are considering changes in work organization or new technologies, differences in inputs, outputs, and work quality would need to be assessed. Obviously, any proposal that improves work quality with no loss in outputs and no investment expense would be noncontroversial since it would improve the national work complex average at no cost. However, whenever investment is necessary to improve work complexes or increase output there must be some way to decide which investments would be sufficiently beneficial to undertake. The national production facilitation board, by estimating per capita growth and anticipated change in the average work complex, provides an initial and regularly updated estimate of the minimal returns needed from investments to make them desirable.

All workers have access to computers on which they can make calculations and comparisons. Returning to our example, after consulting projections, Nancy decides to develop her first proposal for Northstart based on implementing investment plan three.

Nancy must next decide on a level of output—how many titles to publish in the coming year. She could just accept facilitation board suggestions. Or, considering data on population growth, industry IFB predictions of likely growth in numbers of titles desired and in average readership per title, and her own perceptions of people's changing tastes in reading, Nancy could decide industry predictions are a bit too modest and settles on a first proposal to increase titles published by 3.5 percent rather than the IFB projected 3.3 percent, and of readers 1.2 percent instead of the IFB projected 1.1 percent.

To translate her estimates into a full proposal for Northstart, Nancy next settles on number of employees, hours of work per day, and effort levels at Northstart. User friendly computer programs make it easy to enter workplace proposal number three, set a number of titles and readers, and then enter choices for any two of the variables to see what the third must be to get the job done.

It is important to note that the kinds of thinking Nancy has to do become easier with familiarity and, in any event, the programs make the associated calculations simple. In any case, Nancy has arrived at her first round proposal for Northstart for the coming year. What about other workers? And how does a final plan arise?

### The Second Planning Iteration

Not only Nancy but all workers at Northstart and throughout the economy complete their initial proposals and submit these to the "planning data bank." Individuals have made no attempt to accommodate their proposals to one another. But once the proposals are submitted, IFBs work on the data (in ways we discuss in chapter 9) and prepare a report of current proposed supply and demand for all goods including slack components the IFB appends; changes in indicative prices based on relative degrees of excess demand or supply; summary of current averages for consumption and production, and written descriptions of the principal causes of changes in IFB projections.

Of particular importance to Northstart workers are the current proposals for supply and demand of all goods that appear in the Northstart "budget." Therefore, these are highlighted in written reports provided Northstart workers, as are summaries of written reports from consumers regarding books. For example, since consumers are requesting more new titles than the industry suggested producing, the industry receives a written summary of consumer commentary regarding books. We should also note that although Northstart workers and consumers automatically receive this material, they can gain access to similar data for other industries at any time at any computer console in their plant or community.

So if Nancy wishes to see a more detailed breakdown of demand by region or even for specific consumer councils, she can do so easily. She can, for example, use the summary report provided by the iteration boards as a general guide and investigate details for herself, using procedures we describe in chapter 9.

It is important to note that such inquiries on the part of Nancy (or other workers) have more than one effect. In addition to getting feedback important for her planning decisions, Nancy's access to consumer commentary also gives her an indication of the social value of her labors and an understanding of the implications of her choices for others.

Let's return to the planning process. Having noticed that paper is in overdemand and paper producers have proposed no increase in production over last year, Nancy requests a computer printout of the paper industry's own report explaining their proposal.

Then, in response to all the information she has accessed, a new set of indicative prices, and whatever consultations and investigations she wishes to undertake, Nancy makes a new proposal updating her first. The process is the same as the first except she takes

into account new information. We should note, however, that in line with our particular description of this society's planning system, Nancy alters the components of her first proposal in any direction and by any amounts she chooses. The issue, of course, is whether we can expect Nancy in combination with other actors to behave in ways that will bring demand and supply for all items into equality in a reasonable time frame. We address this question in detail in chapter 9 since it involves characteristics of the whole allocation process. But since the indicative prices of goods in excess demand will rise and of goods in excess supply will fall, and since there is social pressure to reduce the overall value of requests (and increase the overall value of output), it is not difficult to see the fundamental mechanism that drives the system toward a match of supply and demand.

### The Third Planning Iteration

After Nancy and everyone else submit second proposals, IFBs again adjust indicative prices, update their own projections, send relevant summary reports to all units, and store all this information in the planning data bank. The new wrinkle is that in addition to industry IFB reports on industry proposals and averages, there are also industry IFB projections for likely final industry plans, as well as suggestions to member units regarding how they might best move toward these likely final outcomes. In instances where a unit diverges dramatically from industry averages, discussions may commence between that plant's board and IFBs to explore the reasons for the differences.

In going over new data and considering how to alter proposals for goods in over-demand or, less often, over-supply, in line with the hypothetical rules used as an *example* in chapters 5 and 6, and since labor reallocations to and from Northstart are already largely settled, Nancy can now only alter her proposals for particular items that Northstart would use or produce by less than 50 percent if she wants to move them in the direction that equilibrates supply and demand, and by less than 25 percent if her proposed change is disequilibrating. And this rule applies as well for developing proposals numbers four through six, discussed below.

Preparing her third proposal, however, also involves Nancy in many more discussions with work mates. While each Northstart worker still makes his or her own proposals for all of Northstart, unlike in earlier rounds they incorporate modifications arising from collective discussion. Thus, one day of meetings in work groups and departments is set aside for discussions of proposals. Like many other details in this discussion, the rules for changing proposals for each new iteration and for carrying out planning within workplaces seem reasonable to us (particularly in societies in which there is considerable friction moving resources from one use to another), but still, these are only *possible* choices included to describe one plausible implementation.

## The Fourth, Fifth, and Sixth Planning Iterations

Now Nancy and her coworkers confront a new challenge: Their fourth proposals will be made not separately but together. The different ideas of Northstart workers must finally be combined into one consistent Northstart proposal. It isn't necessary for each individual's role in the proposal to be spelled out since assignments are irrelevant to the rest of the economy. But workers' councils proposals do need to be implementable. So, although the same limitations on adjustments apply as for the third proposal, now they apply to the *single*, new Northstart proposal.

The formulation of the fourth proposal requires various sessions held intermittently over a full week, though it is certainly not full-time work so that other work also continues. Mainly, a week allows sufficient time for thinking before plant members choose a new proposal.

First the smallest work groups meet and members compare their individual proposals hoping to accommodate them with one another. These meetings serve primarily as a warm-up for more important department and area meetings to come.

Here's how it might work. Nancy has a small group meeting on Monday of "fourth-proposal week." On Tuesday she meets with the editorial department to talk about numbers of titles and readership to try to reach agreement on these matters. On Wednesday, she has a similar meeting with the promotion department, the site of her non-editorial, non-production work. Throughout Northstart, others hold similar meetings, and the Northstart IFB summarizes and distributes each day's results. Monday's meeting is limited to an hour. But those on Tuesday and Wednesday run for an hour and a half in the early morning and then for another hour and a half near the end of the day. In its meeting, Nancy's editorial group begins by listing the number of new Northstart titles each member prefers to undertake, the readership they anticipate, and the mix of different kinds of titles they desire. Debate commences regarding the difference between initial averages of proposals and current consumer demands and projected industry averages. Since each editorial group meets separately, the Northstart IFB reports each group's results as well as an average for them all. The following day Nancy's promotion group starts with the overall average as a premise and suggests its own adaptations in light of promotion needs and potentials. Because all departments do this on Wednesday, there emerges a new average to be considered Thursday. Finally, a council meeting all day Friday functions somewhat like a senate, considering amendments to the average from the floor as a means of developing competing alternatives, and finally voting for one proposal as Northstart's proposal for the fourth iteration.

One important feature of this process would be an effort to accommodate competing perspectives in the form of compromises or experiments. This would allow minorities to present practical evidence of the virtues of their position. The fifth and sixth iterations would proceed like the fourth, but with each taking much less

NORTHSTART
FINAL COORDINATION COMM.

time and incorporating tighter limits on the allowed percentage changes in inputs and outputs. And, of course, for each new proposal there would be new information about the status of goods, average outputs, and indicative prices, all of which would provide pressures to move toward a feasible plan.

## The Seventh Planning Iteration

After receiving the sixth proposals from production and consumption units, industry and national IFBs have a new task: they must consider available data and offer five feasible plans for society to choose among. Since we will discuss IFBs more when we focus on the intricacies of allocation in chapter 9, here we simply assume they do their task well and present society with five proposals. But we should mention that IFB worksheets and minutes of their meetings are available to anyone through computer access. This is to provide units with more information, should they want it, and also to guard against potential IFB manipulation.

Obviously, the choice of *five* plans—like many other details of the process we are describing—could be varied without changing the underlying logic of participatory planning. There could be fewer individual iterations or more collective ones, or limitations on adjustments or submission of council-wide rather than individual proposals could begin earlier or later, and, in a real society such refinements would evolve in accord with particular economic, cultural, and social histories, since once citizens agree that participatory planning has potential, they will modify the system to suit themselves.

In any event, in *our* hypothetical scenario, after a period for discussion and thought, everyone would vote for one of the five proposed plans. The votes would be tallied in each council, submitted to higher level federations as sublevel totals and tallied again, and so on until final results were available—likely within a couple of hours. The two proposals that receive least votes in the first ballot are dropped. IFBs amend the remaining three proposals in light of the relative weight of votes. A second ballot eliminates the least popular of the three. and then the two remaining choices are slightly amended, a final choice is made, and the chosen option becomes the seventh aggregated *projection* of the iteration process. IFBs then use this projection to calculate expected indicative prices, total economic product, growth rate, average work and consumption, and outputs for individual goods, all of which are sent to the plan data bank.

Nancy and other members of Northstart (and all other economic units) now accept the projections for society's total product, average work load, average consumption allowance, and average work complex quality as benchmarks. All further revisions are confined to adjustments of responsibilities within federations and units in light of the overall plan.

# The John Henry Plan

With Northstart planning we emphasized overall logic and left out details of personal discussions and the qualitative dimensions of plan formation. For the John Henry Steel Plant we would like to focus on a few examples of interchanges rather than overall dynamics. This will provide a different slant on the planning process including the types of disagreements likely to occur. It will also help us explain how workers can adjust work loads, and how they pay attention to the qualitative as well as quantitative dimensions of what they produce and use.

## An Overview of John Henry Planning

As at Northstart, planning at John Henry goes through a sequence of iterations involving the evaluation of demands from other units along with attendant proposals, revisions, negotiations, and decisions. John Henry Steel plant employs thousands of workers, has a large amount of heavy specialized machinery, and has a production process that involves an average work complex well below the social average. Proposals for improving worklife at John Henry are therefore high on the agenda, and John Henry workers spend more than the average number of hours doing work outside John Henry at more rewarding labors.

Because the seven planning iterations are formally the same at John Henry as at Northstart, we will not summarize them again. Moreover, since each plant embellishes its own planning procedures with whatever rules, schedules, and divisions of responsibility it chooses, John Henry has many differences from Northstart, but these idiosyncrasies are not our concern here. Instead we want to see some of the disagreements that arise in planning.

## Choosing Between Alternative Production Schemes: An Argument Between Departments

In the early stages of planning John Henry workers must choose proposals to change organization/technology. Let us look in on this process once it has gotten down to a choice between three alternatives.

Proposal 1's main features involve some new furnace equipment and rearranging a few aspects of associated processes. Its supporters claim it will allow a two percent reduction in labor hours per ton of steel output, no significant change in material inputs, and only a modest improvement in the average work complex for the plant by removing one dangerous and one rote task from one part of the production process.

Proposal 2's advocates also claim a small reduction in labor needs and modest improvement in work complex for a similar investment in new equipment. Procedure 2 was proposed by the record-keeping department and affects only work they do. The record-keeping work team estimates a slightly greater improvement in average work complex than for proposal 1.

Proposal 3 evolved through discussions among a number of divisions and involves more elaborate changes including purchase of major new equipment, a substantial redefinition of tasks, and a major rescheduling of plant procedures. It requires a much greater investment and alteration of social relations than either proposal 1 or 2. Its advocates claim it will only marginally increase material inputs needed per ton of steel produced, though it will increase labor needed per ton of steel by three percent. The major advantage of proposal 3 is that it would significantly improve the average work complex at John Henry, offering improved work conditions and increased opportunity for discussion and communication among workers.

Earlier in the planning process a number of other proposals were rejected as inferior, though some of their better features were incorporated into the three proposals. At this point there is a plantwide debate about the three alternatives. Since both proposals 1 and 2 reduce the social cost of inputs without sacrificing output and with only minor investments, there is little doubt other councils in the industry and economy will approve them. On the other hand, since the third proposal requires substantial investment and also increases inputs per output, while the improvement in quality of worklife might warrant the change, this would have to be carefully explained to other units in the economy since the usual "quantitative" indicators would not immediately in and of themselves, indicate grounds for approval.

Advocates of all three proposals have personal biases coming from energy they have invested, pride in having worked out a proposal for their workplace, and heartfelt beliefs. This creates three factions with some overlap, because some workers' complexes involve them with more than one of the departments offering options. For everyone else the only grounds for choosing are a combination of personal preferences and intellectual orientations.

For example, Roger calculates that with either of the first two proposals his situation is likely to change only slightly—work in the plant would be slightly more rewarding and consequently he would probably work fewer hours outside the plant on community day care. The third proposal, on the other hand, would substantially improve the quality of his work at John Henry and lead to a significant reduction in pleasurable outside duties that used to be required to balance his overall work experience. In the short run, Roger expects he would personally benefit considerably, but in the longer run once job balancing committees finished their work, the benefits would be offset by being spread around.

Knowing that equity will be achieved, Roger realizes that for him personally the issue is the same as for society as a whole: which combination of proposals advances well being the most?

Different workers feel more or less strongly about the prospects, influenced by their own circumstances and by their different assessments of implications for others. The decision making process first involves debate and discussion leading to agreement to adopt particular material/qualitative descriptions as the best conjectures about the most likely effects of the three procedures. Although workers can't know for sure how changes in relations or technology will affect them before trying them, they must make estimates or there is no way to proceed with evaluations and choices. Advocates of each proposal present and defend their claims about material and human consequences and, finally, workers vote on the three options. Suppose option 1 gets the fewest votes.

Plant facilitation workers then propose two options which are slightly amended versions of options two and three, and provide spreadsheets that show their anticipated implications. Discussion and debate begins anew. This time, however, a council meeting is convened and works toward resolution in open session. One group of workers proposes a compromise incorporating what seems to be the most popular elements into a single package. A vote accepts this as a better starting place for the forum than either of the facilitation proposals. A period of amending and wrangling commences. At some point workers sense diminishing returns and call for a vote. Indeed, any time the majority votes for closure, meeting time can be reduced, and of course individuals who may reach their personal saturation point earlier can absent themselves from discussions at any point, returning later to vote.

Though some advocates of earlier proposals will likely feel that a second-best choice has been made, everyone understands that what has been decided represents the result of informed democratic deliberations. Everyone congratulates the facilitation workers and proposers of the compromise plan and goes home.

*"Although workers can't know for sure how changes in relations or technology will affect them before trying them, they must make estimates or there is no way to proceed with evaluations and choices. Advocates of each proposal present and defend their claims about material and human consequences and, finally, workers vote on the three options."*

### The Intricacies of "Working Overtime" to Earn More "Income"

Lydia, the reader will recall, lives in a complex whose members are artistically inclined. When not working at John Henry she works with a drama group that puts on plays throughout the region. She likes this so much she spends more time doing it than the time needed to balance her John Henry complex, but since she considers it fun, she doesn't claim it as extra work. However, Lydia wants to get a new computer this year to help her with design and writing for the coming season. She could propose these in the plan as investments for her drama group, but she knows they would not pass since the need is not pressing. Lydia also has the option to "borrow" to make the purchase herself—her Emma Goldman co-housing mates and others in the neighborhood would be happy to oblige this request, especially since her plays provide so much social well-being—but Lydia is not overly pleased with committing herself to "pay back" a loan by consuming less in the future. She prefers to work extra hours now to "earn" the right to the extra consumption right away.

She puts in a proposal to the plant facilitation board requesting sufficient overtime to warrant the extra consumption. She would prefer to take less time for lunch and come in early or work later each day to working on her days off or evenings since that's when she works with her drama group. Once John Henry's plan is settled and the time comes to assign tasks, Lydia's proposal is considered. Confident no one will protest—Lydia works hard, has made few previous special requests, and the John Henry workers are the first to enjoy her plays—facilitation workers assign Lydia the extra time she requests subject to approval by the council as a whole.

Matthew also requests extra work because, like last year and the year before, he wants to ask for an above average consumption bundle. Matthew wants to do the work at convenient times, an extra half hour daily three times a week, for as long as needed.

Facilitation workers doubt, however, that others will want to juggle their work schedules to help Matthew still again, so they ask if he'd be willing to come in Sundays to clean as his additional work. Matthew balks, and his request goes unincorporated into the facilitation board proposal of work assignments at John Henry. Although Matthew later argues his case to the council, its response is the same as the facilitation workers'. He appeals, to no effect, turns down the compromise offer to do overtime on Sundays, and decides to look for a different primary workplace. In the meantime he goes without the above average consumption he wanted.

### Evaluating and "Bartering"

During the period allowed for preparing the third proposal, Sally decides the gap between what the steel industry as a whole has proposed and what consumers have initially demanded is so large that filling the demand would require a significant increase of steel production either at considerable burden to current workers, or by transferring many workers from other areas with disruptive effects. She, like many other steel workers, decides to investigate the reasons for the high excess demand before putting in her third round proposal.

Of course, Sally is quite familiar with how John Henry steel is used. She has a good overview of the whole economy and the role steel plays. She thought the facilitation board's estimate of a three percent drop in demand for this year—given the long term switch from steel to new high-tensile alloys—was reasonable. Therefore, when she first heard it, Sally believed the high demand must have been because some town or city was making a huge request related to a major construction project they would modify quickly seeing the excess demand for steel. She didn't do any serious checking on demand but only on supply to see that John Henry was keeping pace with other plants. But now she becomes interested in components of demand because they must be diverging dramatically from what she expected.

Her first step is to set aside a couple of hours one evening to use one of her complex's main database terminals to conduct her inquiries. Sally begins by calling up statements regarding current proposals for steel supply and demand, including a comparison of current demand proposals with last year's final figures and with the facilitation boards' most recent predictions.

Next, Sally requests a breakdown of demand by industry and region to see the roots of the increase. There could have been a generalized increase in demand for all products requiring steel, but that would contradict the downward trend in steel use. Sally finds that the demand jumps were common to quite a few regions, but not all, and primarily centered in two industries.

Apparently citizens in Northern regions made unusually high demands for automobiles, while people generally were making at least four percent higher than anticipated requests for refrigerators. Because Sally herself hadn't made any such requests she doesn't know what reasons might be at work. With a ten percent increase in automobile requests in the northern regions, it seems likely she could find the explanation with just a few well-conceived inquiries. Thus, Sally next requests a sequence of print-outs including:

1. The average commune and per capita request for automobiles in the relevant regions as well as the national average, the average for other regions, last year's national average, and the projection for this year.

2. A summary of all changes in this year's car models.

3. A similar summary of changes in refrigerators.

With this information, Sally sees that the new model cars have innovations that make them more economical and efficient than last year's models for travel in the cold and snow and she is a annoyed that facilitation workers didn't sufficiently foresee increased demand for new cars in heavy-snow regions.

There is no corresponding improvement in refrigerators that would warrant a four percent jump in demand. Sally asks for a check on reasons people gave in a few representative communes for requesting new refrigerators and discovers an inordinate number of people claiming their refrigerators were out of service. Further research shows that a refrigerator model introduced five years ago is now showing signs of unexpectedly low durability, leading to the unexpectedly high requests for replacements.

In light of her findings, Sally recalculates her own proposals for production at John Henry, scaling things up more than she had initially intended, but not quite as much as consumers sought. She feels the refrigerator need is urgent, but some of the people in the cold regions will simply have to manage without new cars. She also adds her comments to the qualitative data base.

*"There is no corresponding improvement in refrigerators that would warrant a four percent jump in demand. Sally asks for a check on reasons people gave in a few representative communities for requesting new refrigerators..."*

Sally is eager to see whether facilitation board workers will come to similar conclusions in their revised projections for the next round and is gratified when their new projections and explanations are released. They did indeed perceive the same unexpected causes of high demand and elevate their projections for final production of steel only a bit more than Sally had thought warranted.

### Differential Productivity in "Competing" Steel Plants

One of the more interesting differences between John Henry's plan and Northstart's is that John Henry varies dramatically from the productivity norm for its industry. Publishing companies are all able to attain comparable productivity and any publisher producing below average output per input has to have acceptable reasons for doing so. Some steel plants, however, have technologies neither as pleasant to work with nor as efficient in outputs per inputs as others because the yearly fall in demand for steel makes retooling all existing plants inadvisable since the new capacity would just lie idle some years down the road. Instead, selected old plants were only modestly improved in the expectation that before too long the plants would be closed or converted to other uses. The few plants needed to provide the lower steel demand projected for the future were retooled extensively, but other plants like John Henry were only minimally updated. Thus, during the year's planning, John Henry's old technology cannot approach the productivity of the completely retooled plants, or even live up to the industry average.

The point, of course, is that whereas in an employee-managed market economy workers at the old plants would suffer lower incomes due to their plant's lower capabilities, in a participatory economy no such penalty would arise.

# Daily Decision Making at Jesse Owens Airport

The above discussions of Northstart and John Henry illustrate the main contours of *one possible way* of conducting participatory planning within workplaces. Of course, it is not the only way. Other plants might have other rules and methods. There is much room for variation depending on the priorities, interests, inclinations, and circumstances of any workers' council. In any case, making overall planning decisions is not the only sort of policy process required for an economy to work. Every day there are countless choices to make in workers' efforts to meet the commitments they have made. How does all this happen? We can look at Jesse Owens Airport to get an idea of the dynamics.

The plan for Jesse Owens is premised on a projection of the number of customers expected to use the airport each week, which in turn affects staff size, hours of work, shift arrangements, and needs for resources and intermediate goods such as gas for planes and food for patrons. Therefore, changes in the number of people flying, or where they fly, would be the most important reasons for adjustments at Jesse Owens. In any case, having a plan for the year doesn't mean that each day won't involve critical decisions about such things as numbers of people needed at work, numbers of hours of operation, or implementation of innovations. And of course, this must all be accomplished consistently with participatory values.

Jesse Owens Airport chose to divide into units much like those in contemporary airports—shops in terminals, building maintenance, airplane maintenance, flight control and scheduling, passenger meals and other services, and so on. Each unit has its own council whose internal structures may be simple or rather complicated including separate councils for subunits and work teams.

At Jesse Owens, larger councils meet monthly requiring only that representatives attend. Meetings focus primarily on policy problems and difficult personnel questions. When major changes are requested, councils employ the updating procedures discussed in chapter 6 and further in chapter 9.

Day-to-day and hour-to-hour decisions are handled by relevant authorities on the spot. For example, nothing about participatory planning precludes having a field captain of the baggage team at "Rosa Parks Terminal," or a dining coordinator in "Bobby Orr Lounge." Nor does anything prevent these "authorities" from making decisions about short-term scheduling or calls to bring in extra employees. What is precluded is only that such "executive functions" embody levels of authority disruptive of solidarity, variety, or collective self-management. Therefore, these positions would not be held permanently so it would not be the case that some people consistently make decisions for others to carry out.

Decisions about personnel assignments and hiring new workers from applicants or releasing workers to other enterprises where they would be more valuable would be made by personnel committees whose staffs would also have other assignments to balance the quality of their work complexes.

Disputes would certainly arise about such things as irresponsibility, lack of effort, bossiness, etc., so how might these be resolved? Under capitalism, at best such disputes are handled by grievance committees with union reps committed to defending employees no matter what the facts may be, and management trying to get rid of strong union members, intimidate employees, and sanction workers. In coordinator economies, workers have usually been less effectively represented by "official" unions, although sacking even those who do practically nothing is almost impossible. In participatory economies, on the other hand, disputes between workers carrying out administrative and executionary tasks will be settled in committees of other workers who all carry out *both* administrative and executionary tasks themselves as part of their *balanced* job complexes. Of course, different plants might have different procedures for hearing complaints, bringing grievances to councils in cases where principles are at stake, and so on. There are many ways to handle such matters, and choices would obviously be contoured to the particular dynamics of specific workplaces and work forces.

But consider just one issue that would naturally arise at all workplaces on a regular basis—the hiring and firing of employees. There are many reasons for hiring and firing, including an increase or decrease in demand for the product, incorrigible malfeasance by an individual, or replacing someone who has moved on to a new job. There would therefore be movement of people among workplaces in a participatory economy, just as there is in any non-totalitarian economy. How could this be handled?

Each workplace has a personnel committee. Some committee members would mediate interpersonal disputes and problems with employee's work habits, others would process requests to change assignments within the workplace, and still others would process requests for transfer and handle hiring new personnel. Moreover, the last function would be greatly facilitated by industry and regional Employment Facilitation Boards, EFBs. Each workplace would communicate its expected needs for new employees and/or notice of employees wanting to leave to industry and regional EFBs, which would in turn regularly provide information back to personnel committees in workplaces. All this information would also be available on the computer network.

Say that Jackie wanted to leave her job at Jesse Owens Airport in Boston to move South. She would report this to her personnel committee so they would know she was thinking of leaving, and contact the appropriate EFB to enquire about jobs available. Although she could go any time she liked, if she wanted to remain in airport work, then for the benefit of her work mates she might agree to leave in tandem with some other individual's transfer to Boston. Or, more flexibly, she might agree to leave whenever there was an opening she wanted to fill at a southern airport *and* there was a potential employee available to fill her role at Jesse Owens, whether a new worker just out of school, or a transfer from the South, or whatever.

Alternatively, if fewer employees are needed at Jesse Owens the personnel committee would work with EFBs to come up with a list of new places they could confidently apply and organize a process whereby people could decide if they wanted to *volunteer* to transfer. If necessary the personnel committee would also preside over involuntary transfers, although this would usually involve the whole workers' council's approval.

Involuntary transfers would sometimes be necessary in a participatory economy—as in all economies—but they would occur far less often than in other economic systems. First of all participatory economies would not have the type of boom and bust cycles that plague market economies. The need to shift employees would always be a need to move people from one industry or workplace to another due to shifting preferences for outputs rather than a need to lay-off workers in general. Any general decrease in total work required/desired would be shared by all workers in the economy as a welcomed reduction in work hours or work intensity—not confined to a few as dreaded unemployment. Second, balanced job complexes means that much of the pain we associate with transfers is absent in participatory economies. There is every reason to expect more people to be willing to transfer voluntarily since job quality will not suffer in moving. Third, we believe the EFBs would be much more efficient in matching institutions and people than in present economies. While Labor Market Boards in Sweden are head and shoulders above employment agencies and retraining programs in the U.S., the EFBs would have much better information available more quickly, and in particular with much longer advance notice of changes in technologies and long-term investment intentions. In any case, involuntary transfers would never be accompanied by a loss of consumption rights and the social stigma and loss of dignity so common today.

It is a different matter, however, if someone is fired because he or she is unwilling to work, is an alcoholic unable to carry out his or her duties, or is so antisocial that nobody wants him or her around disrupting work relations. It won't do to dodge the issue pretending these problems will never arise in participatory economics. There will be disharmony and disability of diverse types. And there will have to be provisions for dealing with cases that are curable, and others that are not. All we can say is that many of the causes of such behavior will no longer exist in participatory, equitable societies and that we would expect the ways chosen for dealing with the fewer remaining problems of this sort to be far more humane than in present economies.

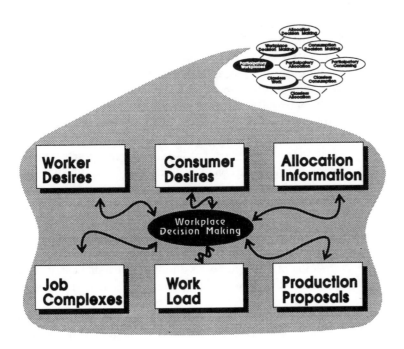

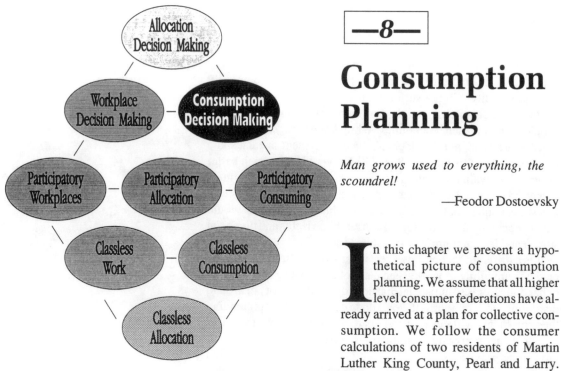

# —8—

# Consumption Planning

*Man grows used to everything, the scoundrel!*

—Feodor Dostoevsky

In this chapter we present a hypothetical picture of consumption planning. We assume that all higher level consumer federations have already arrived at a plan for collective consumption. We follow the consumer calculations of two residents of Martin Luther King County, Pearl and Larry. They behave in what we consider a more or less average fashion.

## Determining County-Level Collective Consumption

Consumption planning begins with collective consumption projects, starting at the highest level and working down, and culminating in a vote on an entire collective consumption package. We look in on this process at the point where actors present requests for county-level collective and individual consumption.

Of course, all of last year's data is available. MLK residents pay particular attention to records of their requests and final plan from last year, to their county's status as a borrower or creditor, to iteration facilitation board projections for this year's average consumption, and to the county consumption facilitation board's summary of collective consumption projects members have suggested.

The CFB would propose various options. But consumers aren't hit with a menu of collective consumption options they know nothing about, have not discussed, and have no opportunity to alter. On the contrary, consumers are periodically informed regarding the formation of these proposals during the year and can intervene at any time with comments, suggestions, and alternative proposals of their own.

Given time to evaluate the various proposals, each living unit discusses the CFB proposals, suggests alterations if it wishes, and registers preferences. Individuals weigh the benefits of proposed collective consumption requests against their estimated social costs as well as estimates of average county consumption within their region. People also consider the implications for individual consumption of collective consumption for which they will be "charged" their fair share.

For example, Pearl who lives with her husband and their three children, a member of Emma Goldman co-housing community, considers how options vary in social costs and benefits. She considers how much a new county cultural center would reduce the need for personal cultural products, what strains would it place on workers and how much would it diminish each county resident's personal consumption budget.

Of course a particularly large county collective consumption request needn't reduce individual consumption budgets drastically in the same period. The "debt to society" can be spread out over time through county borrowing and saving. This is not only reasonable but essential if any large-scale collective consumption is to occur. It would unnecessarily complicate this chapter to incorporate the borrowing and savings aspects of collective consumption, so we assume these "accounting" matters have been taken care of.

In any event, Pearl and others deal with these issues with the aid of the information made available by the CFBs, and computers that quickly and conveniently provide information on the implications for average consumption bundles and make comparisons with other units and past plans. Consumers manipulate software that helps them evaluate the implications of alternative collective consumption choices. For example, Pearl can see data describing how a new community athletic center would reduce allowable individual consumption but permit greater access to exercise equipment, basketball and volleyball courts, pools, etc., for herself, her husband, and her children.

After receiving feedback from all the households that make up the county council, the CFB modifies its list of proposed collective consumption projects and resubmits the list for consideration by households. After a time for discussion, each household ranks the revised proposals, including explanations for its preferences.

At this point, the CFB proposes four possible collective consumption agendas, explaining the implications of each for overall plan possibilities.

Households, co-housing communities, and other living units then vote on the four collective consumption bundles, dropping the least popular with each vote until one remains. This voting is "live"—living units and representatives are linked by computer and TV hookups so that votes can be inclusive and tabulated immediately. In this example as in most other voting procedures, representative structures facilitate making amendments to incorporate as many viewpoints as possible. Then all citizens are able to vote on the amendments because of the speed with which the votes can be tallied.

As emphasized earlier, there is no one right way to undertake collective consumption decision-making. Different counties would employ different procedures.

Once MLK and other counties have settled on their collective consumption requests, they can be summed with state and national collective consumption requests. This accomplished, neighborhood and personal consumption requests can be developed.

## Determining Personal Consumption Proposals

Since neighborhood collective consumption mirrors the logic of county collective consumption, we move to personal consumption requests. To develop a personal consumption plan, Larry consults the IFB's estimates of indicative prices, assessments for collective consumption for members of his neighborhood, average personal consumption estimates, and settles on a "borrower/loaner" status.

To simplify, similar products of comparable quality are grouped together so Larry needs to express preferences for socks, but not for colors or type of socks; for soda, books, and bicycles, but not for flavors, titles, or styles of each. Statistical studies enable facilitation boards to break down total requests for generic types of goods by the percent who will want different types of records, books, or bicycles. There will no longer be competing brands of each product, only "product industries" creating diverse styles and qualities of goods for different purposes.

Larry has under-consumed relative to his allowance in the past two years and has decided to even up the balance a bit this year. On the other hand, his county, MLK, has requested a higher than average county collective consumption bundle, some of which is being borrowed, but some of which will be "paid for" in the present by reducing consumption of MLK residents this year.

Larry knows there is no point being too modest in his initial proposal—the iteration process will compel him to lower his final request as necessary. But he doesn't want to make requests that are outrageously immodest since that would only lengthen the bargaining process and do little to increase his final consumption.

*"People of course have different needs and tastes. But the value of Larry's consumption bundle calculated according to the IFB-generated indicative prices and adjusted for MLK's above-average collective consumption request and his individual status as a borrower against past savings, implicitly expresses what he thinks a reasonable average consumption bundle is for all members of society."*

Larry also knows his selections have social implications. It is not that his choice of a particular kind of food or clothing implies that everyone else should get the same amount of that product. People of course have different needs and tastes. But the value of Larry's consumption bundle calculated according to the IFB-generated indicative prices and adjusted for MLK's above-average collective consumption request and his individual status as a borrower against past savings, implicitly expresses what he thinks a reasonable average consumption bundle is for all members of society. It would be pointless for Larry to suggest a value too far in excess of what the IFB has anticipated, unless he thinks it has made a gross underestimation.

So Larry takes his turn at a computer terminal to try out various combinations of different goods, checking on the total value of his proposed bundle. The computer contains anticipated averages, indicative prices, and so on, as well as descriptions of the products and of the work that goes into their creation. This latter information

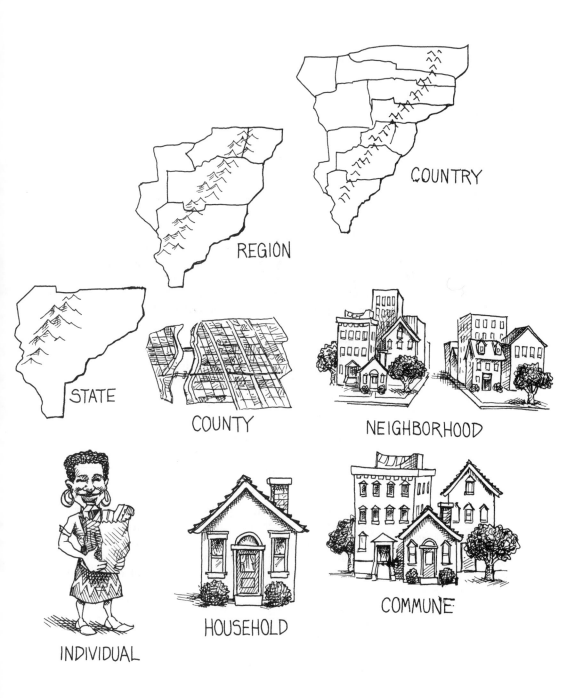

"*Larry knows that if he requests a lot of goods that require work at below-average job complexes, he is implicitly changing the societal average work complex and his own labor requirements. Self interest and collective solidarity argue against such a request unless he thinks the benefits of consuming the good in question are worth the extra drudgery.*"

"*Larry knows that prevalence of consumption requests requiring rote work reduces the quality of society's average work complex and thereby hurts work requirements he himself faces even if he doesn't produce any of the goods in question.*"

helps Larry assess whether rote or dangerous methods must be employed to produce the goods he wants.

Larry knows that if he requests a lot of goods that require work at below-average job complexes, he is implicitly changing the societal average work complex and his own labor requirements. Self interest and collective solidarity argue against such a request unless he thinks the benefits of consuming the good in question are worth the extra drudgery. In any event, detailed information about the production of goods only requires punching a few keys at the terminal.

As Larry completes his first proposal, so do other consumers, and all are submitted to the societal planning data bank where they are summed and processed by IFBs. New summaries are presented including updated projections of anticipated indicative prices, average consumption, and the current status of each good. (We discuss how these new estimates are prepared by IFBs in the next chapter.) Data banks also include summary documentation from each workplace and neighborhood describing the logic of their choices to this point in the process.

Larry, Pearl, and all other members of MLK county go through roughly the same procedure in the second round. They compare their first-round requests to first-round production proposals, see which of the goods they want are in excess demand and consequently have higher indicative prices than originally estimated, and which are in excess supply and have lower indicative prices. They check the value of their overall consumption requests against national averages, talk with their friends, and submit new proposals. Although indicative prices and projected values for average consumption guide decision making, a number of factors refine this relationship. In particular:

a) The quantitative data results from a social process that accounts for gradations in peoples' personal and social preferences.

b) The quantitative data is accompanied by meaningful qualitative information that informs consumers' calculations by providing details about the human sacrifices necessary to produce different goods.

For example, when Larry works on consumption requests he has information about which products embody more desirable work processes and which ones embody less desirable ones. Of course such differences are reflected in the indicative prices of goods, but detailed descriptions of job contents makes this information more humanly meaningful. Larry knows that prevalence of consumption requests requiring rote work reduces the quality of society's average work complex and thereby hurts work requirements he himself faces *even if he doesn't produce any of the goods in question*. He also empathizes with the workers who do produce these goods. Therefore, Larry tries to moderate his requests to emphasize goods requiring more desirable work and de-emphasize goods requiring dangerous and debilitating work.

Therefore, consumers pay attention to the work embodied in the goods they seek because it is in their individual and collective interest to do so, and because it becomes a natural way to behave. Participatory citizens do not have a new human nature nor do economic problems disappear. Rather, the structure of participatory economics has built-in features that promote feelings of empathy such that cooperative behavior becomes as common under participatory economics as competitive egoism is under capitalism.

For the third planning iteration Larry's adjustments are limited, as explained before. But beside limiting changes to less than 50 percent (toward equilibrium) and 25 percent (away from equilibrium) Larry decides to use a convenience *option* available on his terminal. Rather than worry about whether to reduce his demand for something by 14 percent or 22 percent, Larry selects the option that automatically calculates proposed changes for *all* goods toward equilibration at 5 percent (or 10 percent, or whatever he prefers). Alternatively, he might set the automatic global changes in some other pattern he knows to be a good rough fit to his own inclinations. Minimally, he might flag certain items as necessities for him and not subject to reduction (say, electricity) and use the reduction features only on more discretionary requests. In any event, after the automatic changes, he goes through the list of goods and refines the changes for items he wants more precise control over. This approach makes preparing his third proposal very quick, with little loss in quality since Larry makes all final choices himself. Pearl chooses not to employ the automatic feature, spending more planning time for greater flexibility. In any event, after all consumers settle on their choices, proposals are summed, expectations and

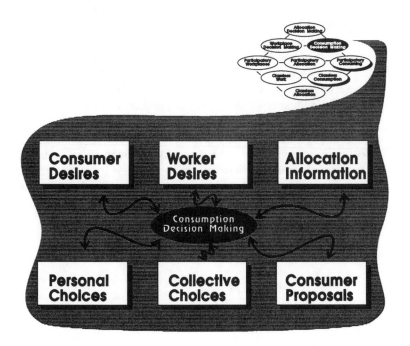

projections updated, and new averages compiled. As in other rounds, each individual submits a new, updated proposal, and these are summed for the commune, county, and society.

In the fourth round, proposals are submitted by neighborhood councils rather than living units. This reduces the burden of adjustments for the planning process and leaves much of the quibbling over living unit requests to the neighborhood councils.

At this stage a proposal might be challenged by neighbors if it's significantly above average in total or if it seems to contain items that may harm the community—such as excessive requests for liquor or drugs.

## Daily Consumption and Changes in the Plan

In chapter 3 we described how consumers would get goods from public stocks and keep track of activities using pocket-size computerized "credit cards." Weekly updating of each individual's consumption would reveal divergences from the individual's consumption plan. These variations might only require a redistribution of goods as some households' increases for a good might be offset by other households' decreases, or increases in demand are met out of slack. Alternatively, it might be that changes in production are necessary or that consumers must moderate their new demands and stick closer to plans they agreed to earlier. In the latter case, consumption council boards would negotiate changes by procedures outlined in chapter 4. In either case, daily and weekly personal consumption allows for privacy, shopping, spontaneity, and changed plans while eliminating the need for bargain hunting and greatly reducing or eliminating hassles of lines and confusion over models, sales, advertising, etc. But the main change, of course, is the elimination of poverty and attainment of equity, goals whose overall implications will only be fully appreciated with their attainment.

Although this chapter's picture of consumer planning is of course incomplete, we hope it provided enough detail to explain how people could participate in planning their own consumption under equitable conditions. Next we consider price calculations and related national accounting.

# 9

# Allocation Decision Making

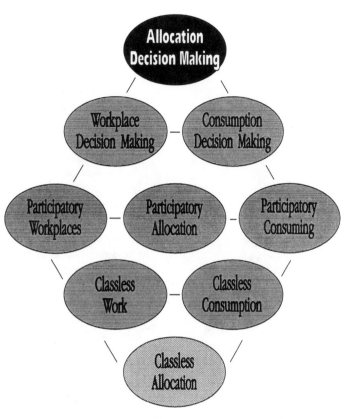

*Who or what institution, except at the centre, can consider the needs of the whole society? What local authority or committee could do so, when it could only have knowledge and responsibility for its own locality? How could the production unit know for whom to produce, what to produce, when to supply it, how it is to obtain its inputs (and from where) unless the planners decide and inform?*

*—Alec Nove*

Having seen how participatory planning works from the perspective of individual production and consumption units, we now address the planning procedure as a whole.

## Developing Initial Data

In earlier chapters we assumed long-run projects were decided before annual planning, and that at the outset of the yearly planning process each economic actor had access to important information. How is this accomplished?

### Long-Run Plans

Should society make a qualitative change in coal mining that drastically improves health and safety, update existing steel plants, build a new high-speed rail line, or transform agriculture to conform to ecological norms? All may be desirable, but presumably given limited resources, not all can be done at the same time. That is the meaning of long-term investment choice and is the problem it poses. Which projects are worth doing and which are not? What order should they be done in? And how fast should we tackle the list, which is to say, how much present consumption are we willing to sacrifice for future benefit?

Long- and short-run investment projects differ in regard to how many years' resources must be committed for the project to reach fruition. Large- and small-scale investment projects differ regarding the magnitude of commitments and the breadth of efforts required. One approach to long-run planning would be to handle this issue before yearly planning begins. At this time, all previously agreed-to long-run projects could be reviewed and updated so that the commitment of resources necessary for this year could become part of subsequent planning calculations. After national projects, large regions could settle on their new long-run projects, and so on, down to the smallest units. In each case, alternative proposals could be aired, preferences expressed, implications assessed, new alternatives broached, options eliminated and improved, and final decisions made, all by participatory procedures similar to those described in our discussion of county-wide planning in chapter 8.

A procedure that could shorten the process would be to first decide the proportion of economic resources we want to commit to investment. Debate about options could then be made knowing roughly how much productive resources were available. Formulation, presentation, and modification of long-run investment options could be made and updated by the investment facilitation boards, who could base their proposals on polls and submissions from units, as outlined in the county example in chapter 8.

It is important to recognize the advantages of collective, participatory, investment planning. In capitalist or market coordinator economies each unit assesses potential investments according to norms imposed by the market and class system. In the workplace, the decision to switch from one technology to another is made by assessing likely profit/loss and capital/labor or coordinator/labor bargaining implications. But this is most definitely not deciding on the basis of social cost and social benefit. Only the benefit of the owner and stockholders is accounted for. Moreover, investment decisions in market economies are not even planned in coordination with one another. For example, the steel plant that decides not to introduce new technology because it appears unprofitable might have decided differently were they able to foresee how innovations in other industries would dramatically alter the cost of inputs or demand for steel.

In participatory planning, on the other hand, coordinated planning in light of social costs and benefits is possible. Each potential investment stands or falls not because of contemporary relationships alone, but because of conditions most likely to prevail once all innovations come on line. Whatever criteria society adopts to determine whether to enact particular investments, the participatory planning system will produce a more accurate assessment of social costs and benefits than would capitalist or coordinator systems. In addition, in a participatory system judgments will emphasize the impact of choices on the whole economy's productivity and social relations from the point of view of improving the quality of life of all workers and consumers, rather than just the circumstances of elite classes.

## *Preparing Data for*
## *the First Round of Planning*

How do iteration facilitation boards estimate overall production and consumption for the coming year? How do they come up with initial indicative prices that economic actors can use, and what exactly do these prices convey? Most important, does proposing likely outcomes and indicative prices make a sham of our claims that no single agent has greater say than others? Can facilitation workers exert undue influence on planning?

Various planning boards begin with last year's results including what inputs generated what outputs in every unit. They know what the final indicative prices were and therefore can calculate the value of last year's production. Moreover, qualitative information is included in extensive reports from all units and federations and quantitative information can be easily manipulated using computer terminals that allow users to see inputs required for any outputs desired.

Facilitation boards modify last year's data to estimate this year's likely outcomes based on comprehensive demographic data regarding likely changes in population by age and gender, the distribution of people between city and country, and so on. They know what investment projects have been completed and how they should affect production potentials. As a result, facilitators can make educated guesses about changes in production work level, and indicative prices.

We could provide more detail, but nothing about this type of data manipulation warrants it. The techniques are well known and noncontroversial—tedious, but not difficult. Facilitators are merely taking last year's data and massaging it in light of projections about investments completed, growth of the labor force, and changes in tastes—the latter being *estimated* from last year's interchanges, and, if desired, polls of particular constituencies.

Facilitators could do their data massaging following only prescribed steps, or with latitude for discretionary and hopefully creative adjustments. In the former case, facilitators' ability to influence outcomes would be nil, but they might provide less than the best possible guesses. In the latter case, there is greater risk of subjective bias, but also potential for better projections. We will talk more about this trade-off later when we discuss examples, but here we make four preliminary observations.

1) It is hard to see any way facilitation board workers (whom we call facilitators for short) could gain by maliciously biasing data even if they went about their work without supervision.

A different but associated problem regarding vulnerability of participatory planning is the question of outright sabotage of the system which might be quite important in the early years of its implementation, if not later. Safeguards protecting against sabotage might well have to be incorporated, but this concern exists in any economy, and arguably, once it has had time to mature, far less so in a participatory economy.

2) The choice between using more flexible but also more subjective techniques and using less flexible but also less creative techniques lies in the hands of society, not facilitation board workers.

3) There is no reason facilitators' discretionary calculations could not be supervised and checked by anyone who wished to.

4) Facilitators' projections are, in any case, only guidelines to help economic actors make decisions.

Facilitators themselves *don't* make *any* production or consumption proposals, *nor* do they revise, veto, or approve any proposals. Indeed, facilitation could be automated with computers taking last year's data and alter it according to rules that tell what changes to make. Facilitators would then only update the program rules as they better understand how variables affect one another. A less rote approach would allow facilitators to use their experience to refine automatic projections. But in either case, facilitators make no decisions about what the economy will do. They only provide information whose formulation is open to public scrutiny and which economic decision makers are free to ignore if they mistrust it.

At the outset of planning everyone in society has access to projections for indicative prices and production and consumption at every level, including summaries of related assumptions. Actors use this information as they please in developing their own plans for the year. It is therefore hard to see how facilitators could bias outcomes even if society chose, as we think it ought to, to give them leeway in their means of calculation and projection.

## Revising Data in Subsequent Iterations

The tasks of facilitation boards in subsequent iterations are not particularly complex. After each economic council and federation submits its first proposal, facilitation boards respond by preparing new data for the coming round. They no longer have to guess based on last year's results. Once this year's initial proposals are in, IFBs calculate the excess demand or supply for every good and adjust the indicative price of each good up or down accordingly. There is room for practical experience and artistry in making the indicative price adjustments or, if preferred, the changes could all be made according to fixed rules. In either case, not every price must be adjusted by the same function of its excess demand or supply. One possibility is that IFB workers with experience in particular industries or with qualitative information indicating whether proposals are relatively soft or hard could expedite convergence by discretionary, informed adjustments. But in any event, in early rounds, IFBs only summarize qualitative information in data banks for councils to assess, calculate excess demand and supply, adjust indicative prices, and revise projections of predicted final outcomes. Of course, the updates of predicted final outcomes are still guesses, but they are based on more information with each new round. Reports of excess demand and supply and qualitative information, however, are a matter of accurate record keeping.

As before, adjustments of indicative prices and projected outcomes could be handled by "automatic procedures" or by allowing greater personal discretion. And again, if we choose to allow more human intervention we would want to guard against bias disturbing the process. But it is possible to make the IFBs' activities as logical and rule-guided as we like and to grant all councils and federations access to IFB deliberations and procedures in any case. We are not urging that all these safeguards be employed. We are merely pointing out that the safeguards are available for those who are nervous about potential abuse.

It is important to note, however, what facilitators would be "updating" in each round. Before planning commences, IFBs use last year's results including information about investment projects, polls taken during the year, and various demographic data to project anticipated results for the coming year. But obviously the actual initial proposals will not be identical to IFB projections. Once this year's planning begins, IFBs are revising information based on the most recent set of proposals actually submitted. So at the outset of round two, workers and consumers receive summaries of qualitative information, new indicative prices, the percentage of excess demand and supply for every good, and new projections of what average consumption and the average social benefit to social cost ratio will be for workplaces this year. Workers and consumers use all this data, as we have discussed, to modify their requests in subsequent rounds.

During the planning process facilitation boards at different levels would regularly communicate with one another and with plant boards regarding logjams, unusual requests that remain far from expected averages, reluctance among producers or consumers to compromise, and especially changing labor requirements that require transfers of workers.

But facilitation boards carry out only communicative tasks; they never make decisions for others. This is not to say that whether they do their job well or poorly, intelligently or myopically, will not affect the final plan. However, as mentioned earlier, it is hard to see exactly what motive IFB workers might have to intentionally bias outcomes, and it is certainly possible to have oversight mechanisms as well.

In later iterations, in addition to adjusting indicative prices and providing new projections, IFBs could generate alternative feasible plans for councils to assess and vote on. Indeed this is the case in the version of participatory planning we have been describing. This approach would increase the potential for IFBs to influence outcomes since in late iterations they would be actually formulating options. It is conceivable, for example, that IFB workers might present five internally consistent plans but not a possible plan that would actually be most preferred. But notice that the only reason for having IFBs present options for a vote is to reduce the number of iterations required to arrive at a final plan. It is a matter of practical convenience, and, should councils be suspicious or unsatisfied with what IFBs present, the councils and federations can always choose to continue the iterative process as they had been. In other words, this stage of the planning process can be postponed until the councils feel that the time saved warrants any diminution in the quality of results. Moreover, the idea is that this time-saving part of the procedure would only begin when the major part of the plan has already been settled on. We are talking about final moves after the essential outcome is no longer in doubt. Moreover, councils could always insist that an additional alternative plan be included with those generated by the IFBs to be voted on.

Finally, we point out to those who fear that computers could become the new dictators, the computer programs are human products, socially evaluated and improved each year. The computer is acting on data and directions emerging directly from the social planning process and the preferences expressed by all actors. The computer uses socially determined data and socially prescribed rules and only carries out data manipulation and calculations. Moreover, and as we indicated, all the "choosing scenarios" we have outlined for producers and consumers allow amendments. In short, neither consumers nor producers need accept computer-facilitated alternatives.

Society could have IFB workers play a substantial role in refining options to embody people's preferences, but as with other procedural choices, there is no one right way. If society chooses a more mechanical approach, the need for special oversight to guard against bias is minimized, but planning might take more time. If IFB workers are given more leeway, as we tend to prefer, the possibility of human error or bias is increased and provisions to correct for it become more important. But workers and consumers probably save planning time.

Whatever combination of automatic procedures and human discretion is adopted for IFB work, unlike in coordinator and capitalist economies, no aspect of participatory planning is immune to critical oversight and social evaluation. Nor is any part of the plan finalized without being filtered through the social barter process where all actors' preferences, evaluations, and opinions interact.

The difference between participatory and central planning is that in the latter, "plan workers" generate the plan, submit it to those who will carry it out, get feedback about whether actors can or cannot accomplish what planners propose they do, and then impose a plan. In our system "plan workers" only facilitate the process whereby workers and consumers propose, haggle over, and revise *their own plan*. And if facilitators formulate any proposals, it is only after all the important decisions have been made.

## Working at a Facilitation Board

Working at a facilitation board isn't much different than working anywhere else in the economy. Work is partly conceptual and partly executionary, and work complexes are balanced by the usual approach of combining diverse tasks. IFB work may be more desirable and more empowering than average work complexes in the economy as a whole, but, if so, greater than average desirability would be compensated for just as it would in any other workplace, by assignments to less desirable tasks elsewhere. Greater than average empowerment, which seems likely, might require rotating people in and out of IFBs after some time period. Likewise, since working at an IFB is particularly likely to enhance people's understanding of the interlocking complexities of economic possibilities, it makes sense to rotate this work, of course taking the efficiency implications of experience into account as well.

## Qualitative Information

In chapters 1 and 2 we emphasized the importance to producers and consumers of understanding the qualitative, human implications for others of their choices. Consumers, we argued, need to be able to assess the implications of their requests for workers. Producers need to know why consumers want what they are working on, not only so they can feel good about their contributions, but also to assess how hard they want to work.

We argued that in addition to quantitative estimates of social costs and benefits, average incomes, and average benefit/cost ratios, producers and consumers also need access to qualitative, descriptive information. In this section we discuss handling this information, a task that might seem daunting.

Consumer and producer councils can easily write up qualitative summaries of work they do and motives for their consumption requests. There is no sense overdoing it. There is no point in everyone saying, "I want milk because it is nourishing." Producers would provide a general description of the quality of work involved in their workplace as well as the desirable and undesirable traits their particular kind of work tends to generate. Consumers would concentrate on explanations of unusual requests. But people trying to assess their own choices in light of other people's qualitative descriptions would want access to summary information at the level of producer and consumer federations. So the tasks are:

1. To develop a data-bank system allowing easy access to all this information.

2. To aggregate the information from lower units into federation level summaries.

Can we imagine an effective way to do this? First, individuals would need "keys" to extract qualitative information. I would go to a console, and say, "Let me see what goes into producing such and such good," or "What is work like in such and such an industry?" or "What is generating the high consumer demand for refrigerators?" or "Why does a particular neighborhood want so many more than the national average?" We could also ask, "What are the strengths and weaknesses of such and such a product?"

If we think of all the money spent yearly in the U.S. on advertising—most of which is misinformation—we can see that the information system we need may not be such a burden on time and resources after all. Indeed, it may require significantly less than the total resources and energies currently alloted to less comprehensive and less truthful, though more repetitive and wasteful advertising.

Though the information-handling capabilities of such a system would have to be quite powerful, only the system's scale distinguishes it from data-bases already used in offices all over the country. The problem of storing and accessing descriptive information is nothing new for programmers, nor is establishing a rote system for updating or otherwise refining such a database, giving it a simple query system, or having it provide averages. Moreover, even for a large country, the system we need would not require much more memory and handling than current systems for large credit-card companies.

For the most part, IFBs would oversee the qualitative data-base system. Summarizing large numbers of individual reports would be demanding, but like other tasks it could be organized to minimize the likelihood that IFBs would bias the information councils use.

## The Logic of Participatory Planning

Any economy must have a method for allocating goods and resources. Different ways of accomplishing this will naturally have different implications for who does what, who gets what, and what will be produced, consumed, and invested.

Someone committed to the view that civilization is best served by pitting people against one another will opt for allocation via competitive markets. Someone who thinks complicated decisions are best made by experts who should be materially rewarded for their expertise will opt for central planning. In either case, according to most economists these are the only feasible allocation procedures. We claim this "impossibility theorem" is little more than self-serving prejudice and to prove it we have tried to spell out how consumers and producers could participate equitably in planning and in coordinating their joint endeavors—*without* central planning and *without* markets.

Are people capable of taking control over their own lives, caring for one another, and acting to enhance their own situations and the situations of their fellow citizens? Can we have an allocation system that promotes solidarity by providing information necessary for people to empathize with one another and by creating a context in which people have not only the means to consider one another's circumstances but also the incentive to do so? Can we have an allocation system that promotes variety at the same time that it creates balanced complexes and egalitarian consumption opportunities tied to effort? Can we have an allocation system that promotes collective self-management by permitting every worker and consumer to propose and revise her/his activities? Can we develop an allocation system that promotes equity rather than class division and hierarchy?

We think other economists deny that all this is possible because to admit that people can conduct their economic affairs in these ways undermines rationalizations for all forms of existing privileges whereas historically it has been the job of economists to rationalize these privileges as inevitable.

Economic activity can be made equitable by ensuring that desirable and undesirable tasks are shared equally. Fulfilling and rote work can be mixed to create equitable work complexes. Consumption bundles can be balanced to ensure roughly equal access to consumption opportunities. Decision making authority can be assigned more or less in proportion as decisions affect people.

Ironically, deep prejudices based on years of experience in oppressive circumstances make seeing all this as a real possibility the most difficult step in the journey to a better economy. Those who hesitate to undertake the tasks of designing such an economy do so not because the tasks are so difficult, but because doing so challenges ingrained prejudices and undermines elite interests.

*"Ironically, deep prejudices based on years of experience in oppressive circumstances make seeing all this as a real possibility the most difficult step in the journey to a better economy. Those who hesitate to undertake the tasks of designing such an economy do so not because the tasks are so difficult, but because doing so challenges ingrained prejudices and undermines elite interests."*

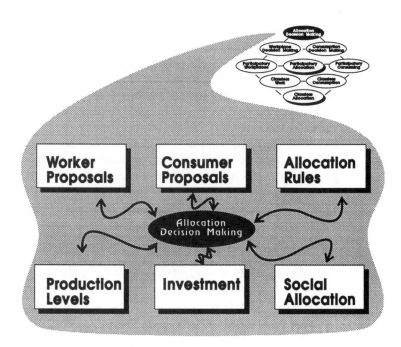

# 10

# The Information Society

In our discussion of participatory economics, computer systems have been described as important tools for furthering democracy. We know, however, that many reasonable people fear computers as weapons of "big brother." On what grounds do we trust these machines that many libertarians loathe? Are there pitfalls we have overlooked? Can we really use computers developed for double-entry accounting and missile tracking to facilitate liberatory social relations in a participatory society? Is our vision of a desirable "information society" really an alienated hell where emotions are reduced to statistics stored in a jumble of wires and chips?

## Technology and Economic Relations

Some believe that all tools are neutral, neither intrinsically good nor evil but only made good or evil by the ways we employ them. We use gunpowder to kill one another or to clear fields for planting. The way we use tools determines their worth.

Indeed, objects have utility only in a particular setting as used by particular people. One can even use an electric shock machine to dim lights or as a paperweight rather than to mutilate people. Out of context, the lump of metal and wires has no positive or negative features. It just is.

But once we notice how much more it costs to produce a shock machine than a light dimmer or paper weight and the social relations of the society in which it is produced, we know a shock machine is not a neutral tool. A shock machine carries the stamp of a social malignancy. It is an irrational tool for dimming lights, for holding down paper, or even for cardiovascular treatment to sustain life. It is a good tool for torture. In the real world this machine is not functionally neutral.

Capitalist societies have created complicated technical means for performing countless tasks. How many of these technologies cannot sensibly serve humane purposes in an alternative society? How many embody capitalist norms antithetical to liberatory goals and should be abandoned?

Take energy production. Many technologies operate in ways that are no more capitalist than participatory—light bulbs built to last, radios, jigsaws, and elevators. Other technologies have built in anti-participatory implications for social relationships or the environment. For example, we will not have nuclear fission reactors in an established participatory society because these reactors require a degree of administrative and decision-making centralization antithetical to democracy as well as ecological risks antithetical to concern for human life.

Moreover, many machine tools and assembly-line technologies will also disappear under participatory economics because their "effective" use would preclude participatory organization by *requiring* hierarchical divisions of command, inflexible social relations, ecological decay, or other social ills.

But before treating the more complicated case of computers, we should review just how technologies come into being in different societies.

## "Darwinian" Technological Evolution

The idea that a technology bears the stamp of the society that spawned it has a Darwinian flavor. In biology, new qualities produced accidentally by a genetic mutation either survive and multiply or die off and have no lasting effect. If a genetic alteration survives, it will be because the mutated host has survival advantages over brethren that don't have the new quality. The lucky organism's progeny pass along the new traits, and their progeny do the same. The altered offspring survive at a higher rate than organisms with old traits. In due course only descendants of the first organism that enjoyed the mutation survive. Two features of Darwinian logic from biology are relevant to "technological history."

First, genetic innovation spreads if it enhances the host's probability of survival in the host's environment. If a new trait increases the likelihood of the host passing on its genes to descendants, it will *likely* spread—though the mutated host could get eaten before ever having any offspring. But luck or not, if the new trait hampers the host's chances of surviving, it will not spread.

Second, a genetic accident that creates new qualities $xx$ and $yy$, which enhance the probability of survival may also create qualities $aa$ and $bb$ that have few implications for survival in the current environment but could become important in another environment. Many human mental capacities were not selected because they would allow humans to master math, physics, or engineering as these were irrelevant capacities in the environment in which these traits were selected. However important they eventually became, these were only byproduct capabilities that became relevant to survival (or extinction) much later, in greatly changed environments.

Now consider technologies. Someone invents a new way of doing something. If the new technology is useful enough to people who have the means to implement it, it will become commonplace. If it is practically useless or if it is useful only to people who have no means to implement it, it will likely disappear.

Our society is full of technologies that were useful to people who were in a position to give those technologies an "evolutionary advantage": assembly lines, cars, power plants, radios, telephones, disposable razors, atomic bombs, guided missiles, personal computers—ad infinitum. But we can also think of a host of efficient technologies that were unsupported— effective public transport systems, efficient large-scale solar energy systems, cars that get superior gas mileage, quality inexpensive housing, and production techniques that empower workers. All these unsupported technologies have been invented and some prototyped, but they haven't succeeded in our economic environment because they were not advantageous to those who decided their fate. They didn't fit in the environment of capitalism or in the environment of centrally planned systems, for that matter.

No technology evolves and spreads unless there are people who benefit from it and have sufficient means to disseminate it. In a capitalist society, technologies useful to the rich and powerful spread. But this doesn't imply that every technology developed in capitalism is useful only to capitalists or other elites.

Consider television. It has been useful to capitalists, men, and members of majority communities because television has been used to disseminate vast quantities of disinformation promoting capitalist, patriarchal, and racist interests, distorted our view of social good and bad, fostered rampant consumerism, and generally fostered a passive lifestyle. Yet even in capitalism television sometimes provides good entertainment, educational information, and occasionally important news, all of which benefit everyone. Moreover, in a different social setting that supports democratic two-way communication, television *could* serve many useful purposes. Unlike shock machines, nuclear reactors, and some assembly-lines, TVs needn't be dumped in the ashcan of history along with authoritarian, patriarchal, racist, and classist institutions and relations. Instead, TVs could be put to good use in a participatory future.

We could even imagine circumstances in which attributes of "participatory television" might begin to be elaborated within a capitalist setting because they might also serve certain capitalists' ends. For example, two-way TV might profit some capitalists (for example, by use of shop-at-home schemes) at the same time as they begin to serve citizens in ways contradicting broader capitalist interests. Powerful pressures would then arise to try to curtail the "anti-capitalist" side of these developments, but these efforts might in turn be opposed by citizens seeking to enlarge the liberating effect of new techniques. Are computers like televisions or like shock machines?

## Special Characteristics of Computers

The computer itself is merely an array of electronic circuits that store data in the form of switches that are either on or off and that change their status as directed by a program or user.

As a user I put in data. The computer translates the characters I type (or the words I speak) into patterns of switches either on or off. I direct the computer to perform a function on the data, and the computer responds by changing its switches. I receive the result on the screen, a paper print-out, or a computer disk, and that's all there is to it.

What is remarkable about a computer is the fantastic speed with which it can manipulate vast amounts of data and diverse types of information—especially when we consider that all that really happens is that switches turn on and off in changing sequences.

If we want to store a number the computer must translate it into a pattern of ons and offs in a particular set of switches. Once upon a time the operator typed in very detailed instructions that listed the names of the switches and told them what to do in a highly arcane code. Today, though codes like this are still the language that ultimately instructs the computer, operators use familiar words and phrases which the computer translates step by step into its own "machine language."

In any case, if we want to add two numbers that we have stored, we must provide the computer with instructions that, when turned on by a user, will combine the two sets of switches representing the two numbers to create a new pattern of ons and offs. The new pattern represents the sum of the numbers. While we can do this just by saying, "Add 17 and 483," what the computer does in response is even more tedious than it appears.

For example, imagine the endless sequences of switches involved in solving a difficult equation predicting stress lines for a bridge design or the flight trajectory of a missile. We are talking about millions upon millions of minuscule electronic switches changing every second. The number of steps needed to get a result makes an abacus look high-tech. But in speed per step, computers are unparalleled.

The same on-and-off patterns can represent letters, spaces, and punctuation marks that the computer manipulates when an operator punches combinations of typewriter keys labelled with such commands as "erase a line" or "move a paragraph." Again, all the patterns of ons and offs must be meticulously manipulated to create new patterns representing the newly processed text. In addition, the computer must be able to tell a screen or printer to display recognizable letters based on these switch patterns. Again, it is all unrelentingly tedious.

If people did mathematical manipulations or text processing by mimicking the steps undertaken by computers, they would never get anything done. The computer's approach involves far too many steps for each operation. But computers are so fast that they can manipulate numbers millions of times faster than the fastest mathematician. And this speed is so amazing, it often looks like computers actually think better than we do.

If you ask an astute student to add all the odd numbers that aren't divisible by three and are bigger than 11 but smaller than 201, he or she will take at least a few minutes to do the job, thinking all the while. But a properly programmed computer will take the smallest part of a second to do the same task. Or if you ask a writer to count the number of words in a book and then list them alphabetically including the number of times each is used—well, you can imagine how long that would take. Yet even a contemporary desktop computer can do this in minutes, including looking up all the words in a dictionary to find typos and misspellings. Does it think that much better than we do?

No. In fact, the computer doesn't think at all, ever. The computer plods. It electrically alters arrays of switches according to precise, unbreakable methodical rules. No more.

But the computer does this so quickly it seems to think at lightning speed. High powered computers solve problems in days that teams of top mathematicians would struggle over for multiple lifetimes. Even today's desktop computers allow college students to perform in an evening all the calculations that dozens of mathematicians would have grappled with for weeks a few years ago. But the computer doesn't think as well as even one of those mathematicians, or, by any sensible standards, even as well as a dog or a chipmunk or pigeon. Perhaps one could argue that the average computer has an intelligence quotient competitive with that of an inch-worm or some such creature. But that's all. What the computer is, however, is fast.

Give a chess player a board with a midgame position and ask her to pick a move. After a few moments, depending on her ability, she will have one. She has calculated patterns of possible moves—if I do this, what might the opponent do and how do I like the result— but mostly she has intuitively honed in on the most likely type of move that should be made. The good player, in particular, will examine only a few different options because she will intuitively close in on a good move just by "feeling" the position's character.

Asked the same question, however, the computer calculates the pattern mechanically according to predetermined unchanging rules put in by programmers who did all the thinking. But it does this for many more options—perhaps a million more per second—than any player would ever dream of considering. The computer doesn't make the intuitive leaps of even a middling player, but nonetheless the best computers can already beat all but a very few human players.

Computers do what we tell them, very quickly. They do not intuit or think. Perhaps the best indication of this is, ironically, that computers do not make mistakes. There are no wrong analogies or computer leaps of logic that lead to wrong results. Computers simply follow orders without knowing what they are doing, just as a radio follows "orders" to play louder or softer without *knowing* what "louder" or "softer" means.

If we tell a computer to solve a difficult equation for some variable, it does not think about the equation and assess it, but instead rushes, willy-nilly, to solve it by a series of steps preprogrammed by a human programmer. If a student tried to solve problems this way, he or she would fail most of the time. But the computer rarely fails.

So, computers can be used to store and speedily manipulate mathematical and linguistic data according to any rules programmers can embody in computer "software." For a long time it seemed that computers would only be good at dealing with numbers. If this had been true, it would have meant computers could only be used to answer questions that could be quantified. In a workplace, therefore, we would use a computer for storage and manipulation of quantifiable data. Having a computer might even propel us to rely increasingly on quantitative calculations to the exclusion of qualitative considerations, since the latter would be too difficult to manipulate on the computer.

And in fact, however we refine computers, it is true that there will always be a difference between their quantitative and qualitative capabilities. For the former, the computer can do every kind of logical manipulation that people can, only much faster. For the latter, however, though the computer can store qualitative information in the form of words or pictures, it cannot manipulate the represented values, judge them, compare them, or extrapolate from them in even a fraction of the ways humans can. Computers can help people do these tasks but cannot do them in place of people.

Another criticism of computers is that they are not "the real thing." When we communicate through computers we are not communicating directly, or when we play simulated games on computers we are not playing the real games. But this is only a problem in one sense. It is true that if we use computer communications and simulations to take the place of accessible human communications and real-world experiences, then the "unreality" of computer activity becomes negative. But if we use computers to facilitate something akin to human interaction *where otherwise there would be no interaction*, and something akin to real experience *where otherwise there would be no experience*, then the computer can enhance communication and experience.

A last and more subtle complaint about computers is that people tend to bestow them with unwarranted authority. It is likely a complex product of modern culture and personality types that people seem disposed either to hate and fear computers, or, having gotten over that, to attribute to them almost unlimited capacity for accuracy. Both reactions have a basis in fact, of course, but both are also exaggerations.

Regarding hate and fear, the issue is the extent to which computers are harbingers of justice and pleasure, or of surveillance and alienation. The rest of this chapter addresses this, so let us pass on it for the moment. Regarding computer accuracy, we need to say something here.

If we are asking computers to make calculations, no matter how complex, it is reasonable to have faith in the answers we get assuming that the program is well tested and debugged though in many cases this is a difficult task and the possibility of "bugs" should not be minimized. But if we are using a computer simulation to try to understand a complex real-world situation and predict its possible responses to human interventions, much *more* care is called for. Just because we think we have written a program that embodies all that is important about the workings of a nuclear plant or an economy, and we think the program has been successfully debugged, we should not be overconfident that when the screen tells us the plant will always be safe or the economy will never exceed ten percent unemployment this will prove true.

Computer simulations are based on *models* of real phenomena, which must capture *all* the elements of reality relevant to outcomes we are interested in if they are not to be misleading. If we do not understand the phenomena fully enough to capture *all* these elements, or if we are ideologically constrained from capturing all these elements, then no matter how accurately we transfer the model into a computable scheme and no matter how efficiently and elegantly we write the code for its program, the computer will yield incomplete and thus inaccurate projections. This is no different than the simple and obvious truism that whenever anyone tries to predict how a situation will change in the future, he or she does so based on assessing some number of variables in light of some beliefs about how their status affects future trajectories. If these beliefs are wrong or if important variables are left out, we get wrong answers. Likewise for the computer. The problem is that with people we anticipate this fallibility. With computers, if we become entranced with their power, we tend to forget this fallibility, especially when they tell us what we want to hear—of course because we built what we want to hear in the model they are using. The only solution is caution induced by recognition of the limitations of model building.

Important as these considerations are, ultimately computers deal only with information. And it is the quality of this information, not computers, that makes the so-called "computer revolution" a possible thrust toward greater democracy. For unlike many products of human labor, information does not come in clumps so that if you take some there is less left for me. Once anything is known, we can all know it. There is nothing to run out of. Once an idea exists, there is enough for everyone. We need only distribute it. The potential democratizing character of computers derives from the possibility that computers may elevate information as the main currency of social life, so there will no longer be a scarcity of the most important determinant of well-being.

But is this an inevitable outcome of the production and dissemination of computers? Will democracy necessarily expand with universal availability of knowledge? Or does it depend on what kind of society we put all these computers to work in? Is it possible to preclude most people from access to computers and information even if there is little or no social cost to providing access for everyone? Worse, is the information-age rhetoric a hoax obscuring the fact that computers lead inexorably toward more inequality, more hierarchy, and more poverty of means of expression for some alongside a growing abundance of means of expression for others? To answer these questions, we must consider computers in the context of specific social systems.

## Computers and Capitalist Economics

Computers were born and developed under capitalism. How have computers served the interests of those with the means to promote their spread? And what subversive byproduct capacities, if any, do computers have?

Under capitalism, owners and managers are eager to use new technologies that can mystify work, disempower employees, and replace potentially rebellious workers with machines that don't talk back. Similarly, technologies with military applications are welcome in militaristic societies and technologies that strengthen surveillance techniques are welcomed by those atop all kinds of hierarchies. In short, if a new technology can help dominant elites maintain their advantage, it will be promoted by those elites. Even a cursory survey of the history of computer advances makes clear their overwhelming dependence on military financing.

Obviously—when armed with software that replicates rote human behavior, that accelerates functions essential to profit-making, or that allows data retrieval critical to social control, military radar, or targeting—computers meet the needs of capitalists, politicians, and military elites well placed to promote their production and dissemination. Promoted by these interest groups, it should be no surprise when computers disenfranchise workers by further fragmenting production tasks, allowing more effective oversight and control, fostering the use of new kinds of equipment, and making weaponry even more lethal.

Computers are "mutations" *potentially* well suited to the environment in which they were born. If further development and dissemination of their hardware and software is regulated so that no disruptive characteristics emerge, certainly computers will reproduce patterns of life familiar to capitalist, racist, sexist, and authoritarian societies.

But what if the development of computers takes a different turn? What if, in addition to features that appeal to the various elites of contemporary societies, they also have byproduct capabilities serviceable to oppressed groups? Indeed, even in the U.S. we can see emerging uses for computers that seem contrary to the reasons why elites championed them in the first place.

At the level closest to the top, some technocrats are beginning to argue that computers would allow *them* to greatly streamline social functions if only restraints currently imposed by property owners could be removed. Further down the hierarchy, hackers are poking around in data banks of companies whose owners *and* managers want privacy. Increasingly aware of how easily it can be provided, employees are demanding access to computer records—partly to make more strategic demands regarding pay and conditions, partly because they think they might be able to do a more humane job of running their workplaces than their employers.

Some people are already talking about computers allowing a decentralization of decision making and redefinition of job patterns. The millions who own personal computers are developing important skills capable of demystifying the work of intellectuals. Will there be computerized distribution of books and journals to all citizens under capitalism? If yes, then everyone will have easy access to vast amounts of information and knowledge. Will large numbers of people become familiar with how computers work and develop some programming capabilities? If yes, it will be harder to use computers to mystify illegitimate authority. Unless most people can be prevented from attaining this access to computer technology—a real possibility in the contemporary U.S.—this could certainly be a subversive development.

Are these liberatory potentials subversive of capitalist relations insignificant when compared with the mystifying and fragmenting effects of computers? Or are they significant byproducts that could abet important changes in social relations? A lot depends on how social groups other than capitalists and political elites struggle to define the uses and distribution of computers.

In the worst scenario, computers will become a tool of repression and regimentation in an Orwellian future. They will make thuggish fascism obsolete by making slick fascism more effective. Everything anyone reads, owns, or says will come under big brother's scrutiny. But this needn't be the case.

## Computers and Coordinator Economics

The major difference between capitalist and coordinator economies is that in the former the currency of economic power is property, while in the latter it is information. In capitalism, the ruling class rules because it owns the material means of production. In a coordinator economy, control over knowledge empowers the coordinator economic elite. In the coordinator economy, whether allocation is by central planning or markets, coordinators are responsible for the vast majority of economic decisions. They monopolize information critical to making decisions and skills associated with controlling hierarchical work settings. They also claim a disproportionate share of society's produced output for themselves.

In many ways the uses of computers in coordinator societies are similar to their uses under capitalism, though in the former case the coordinator class no longer functions at the behest of a class of owners. As economic chieftains they work not to maintain property relations and profit margins for owners but to maintain their own monopoly on information and skill as their means of appropriating a disproportionate share of social output and power. Like capitalism, coordinator economies can come in more or less totalitarian forms. To date we have seen the more totalitarian versions in which most intellectuals and professionals are excluded from access to most important information. While many of these coordinator societies are currently reverting to capitalism, it is still unclear where the Soviet Union and China are headed. And, in any case, if social democratic trends persist, we may see transitions from more to less authoritarian coordinator forms in Europe's future. The point is that computers can fit into this setting even if they are accessible to all intellectuals and administrators, so long as they are kept from other members of society.

So whereas capitalists want computer science to advance the old capitalist goals, coordinators want computer science to rationalize society under the sway of mystified knowledge they monopolize. The two economic systems have different characteristics. But neither serves the interests of ordinary workers and in both computers are primarily tools of elite control. From the workers' perspective the struggle between coordinators and capitalists is ultimately a fight between two factions of the "haves." The struggle could be over whether massive advertising and aggressive marketing, as at IBM, or technocratic creativity in product design, as in smaller companies, will determine success in high-tech industries—a very interesting contemporary example of coordinator versus capitalist struggle *within* capitalist society—or over economic structures themselves. But what if the non-elite began to struggle over the definition and dissemination of computer technologies? What difference might that make?

## Computers and Social Change

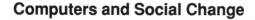

Insofar as people use computers to better understand their work and use that knowledge to demand control over their own lives, they are moving in a participatory direction. When workers want access to accounting records, when homeowners want access to bank and city council records, and when everyone seeks cheaper access to greater quantities of knowledge, this propels participatory developments.

As we have seen, in participatory economies, computers are employed to amplify the quantity and usefulness of information reaching everyone, thereby facilitating decentralization of decision making. Computers in participatory economies can help streamline

communications, enrich cultural and political discourse, and generally democratize society. The computer is a remarkably malleable tool. Depending on the software used, it can be molded to countless uses. The process can be democratic and free or programming can become a new priesthood.

If capitalist relations persist, computer technology will continue to be relatively inflexible and centrally controlled by a small coterie of experts loyal to capitalist employers. If the "servants" get out of hand, the technocratic priesthood can embark on fascist endeavors of their own.

If traditional coordinator systems survive, computer technology will be developed to further centralize and protect important information, even from most of the elite who are trained to use it. If more democratic coordinator relations are introduced, computer technologies may be accessible to 15 percent to 30 percent of society. Even so, the majority would experience computers primarily as a tool of oppression, even if they were better cared for by coodinator planners than by their prior capitalist masters.

But if humanist social relations are introduced, computers will become a democratic tool employed to promote nonhierarchical participatory economic, gender, community, and political relations.

In any case, in today's societies computer technology is one area of struggle between social groups seeking different futures. Depending on who defines their use and development, computers will promote capitalist, coordinator, or participatory goals. Capitalists and coordinators don't yet have complete mastery over the newest technological revolution—though they certainly have a leg up on the rest of us. But if we launch campaigns that touch society's democratic nerve, computers can become a positive force for the better.

# 11

# Conclusion and Transition

*It is necessary with bold spirit and in good conscience to save civilization.... We must halt the dissolution that corrupts the roots of human society. The bare and barren tree can be made green again. Are we not ready?*

—Antonio Gramsci

I n the book you've just read we've described many details of a new economy, but of course much is still missing. Occasionally we have dealt implicitly with an issue, but no explicit treatment appears. Other times, undoubtedly, we haven't had the foresight to recognize issues. More important, economics isn't everything and we have said practically nothing about kinship, culture, politics, ecology, and international relations. Here we note some of "what's missing" that requires further work.

## Economics

T here are many alternative approaches to organization and decision-making that might be employed in different versions of participatory economics. We have offered only an example or two in each instance. But there are other matters as well. One important question is whether there should be special institutional features to safeguard the ecology. Will self-management and the new motivations of participatory planning suffice? Or will additional structures be needed? Suppose people need to evaluate a major investment with long term environmental benefits but which makes contemporary work more onerous. In participatory planning each actor has a say proportionate to the effect he or she feels. Who speaks for future generations?

Or suppose we discover in the year 2029 that a particular computer monitor damages the optic nerves of its users. Are people who used the monitor entitled to compensation? Should the planning process reassess work complexes for prior years and award those who worked with these monitors better than average complexes until equity is attained? If the answer is yes for the health-damaging monitors, what about less extreme cases? Must there be a continual regrading of everyone's past contributions and recalculation of future responsibilities so that everyone bears a fair burden and enjoys a fair return in light of *corrected* evaluations of job complexes?

We also did not address the issue of children's budgets and economic rights. Should each additional child entitle his or her parent, parents, or guardians a whole new budget allotment or only a partial one? Should the size of the additional allotment vary with the age of the child? Should retired workers get a full budget allotment? What are the implications of different options for people's incentives to have children or retire? If dependents have rights regarding how their budgets are spent and if guardians/parents violate those rights, what recourse do dependents have? Could these matters be handled differently in different cultures or locales, or is only one solution consistent with equity, self management, and variety?

While we have described many aspects of a participatory economy, we did not model participatory planning mathematically or prove "convergence and efficiency properties." We refer readers concerned that it is impossible to generate indicative prices with the properties we claim for them, or that convergence and efficiency could not be achieved via participatory planning, to our companion volume, *The Political Economy of Participatory Economics* (Princeton University Press, 1991). There we provide rigorous proofs of "convergence and efficiency properties" under diverse assumptions and discuss the relevance of conclusions based on such models. Similarly, we have not spent as much time as some readers might wish distinguishing our model from other more familiar systems based on central planning and markets. But the companion volume does this and we saw no need to repeat the arguments here.

We also refrained from reviewing historical experiences that bear on the feasibility and desirability of participatory economics. Yes, the discussion of Northstart Press is based on experiences of South End Press, this book's publisher, where, within the limits imposed by operating in a capitalist economy, participatory economic principles and procedures are enacted. But what about Mondragon in Spain, or the experience of the Spanish anarchists before the Second World War? What about experiments undertaken in China, Cuba, the Soviet Union, and Poland? What about employee-managed enterprises, cooperatives, or experiments in communal living in the U.S. and elsewhere? These undoubtedly harbor lessons that could help refine participatory economic vision. Examining such experiences to further understand economic equality, self management, and variety should, therefore, be a worthwhile undertaking.

A final critical matter addressed without practical evidence being offered is whether a participatory economy will really work. To verify a vision's worth certainly entails thinking hard about the vision and its components in the manner undertaken in this book. But before embarking on a full-scale construction involving a new physical or chemical design, serious people not only think hard about the situation, they also do experiments with simulations and/or scale models or partial implementations. Following the same pattern, ways should be found to run simulations and to implement parts of participatory economics to test hypotheses about its rules and behavior and to verify its predicted features. Yet we have said little about these types of verification in this book. Moreover, in our companion volume, *The Political Economy of Participatory Economics*, while we describe a methodology for undertaking experiments and simulations, we do not undertake the tasks themselves. This work remains to be done.

A particularly useful and manageable task would be to create a computer simulation to mimic the operations of a participatory economy. This would permit testing the effects of different assumptions about consumers' and producers' preferences and behaviors, different rules for revising proposals, different procedures for calculating indicative prices, etc. Such a program might also allow individual users to interact on their own PCs as if they were a consumer or producer in a participatory economy planning their economic involvements for a year. This could make more tangible the activities involved in participatory planning.

## Extra-Economics

Imagine a society with a participatory economy but a sexist kinship sphere. That is, suppose that most work associated with maintenance of living units and bringing up children was still done by women. What would happen? If households were treated as economic units, the principle of balanced complexes within units would conflict with this sexist division of tasks. Sexism would have to disappear or the norms of participatory economics would have to be jettisoned.

Alternatively, however, if housework and child-rearing were deemed personal responsibilities not subject to the norms of participatory economics, a sexist division of kinship activities would subject women to double duty—a full and equal share in the economy and child-care and housekeeping as well.

Participatory economic and sexist kinship arrangements might co-exist for a time, but the effects of participatory economics on actors' personalities, capabilities, and values would undermine sexist violations of equality, self management, and variety in the home. In reverse, however, the effects of sexist kinship relations in the home and families would subvert equality, self management, and variety at work and in consumption. In short, the institutions and roles in two critical aspects of social life would have contradictory implications for actors' attitudes so that in due course either one or the other would alter.

Once this reciprocity is understood, it becomes clear that the problem of building a participatory economy is intimately linked with the problem of building a feminist kinship sphere. Moreover, the same reasoning applies to issues of politics, race, culture, ecology, and international relations. Therefore anyone seriously interested in attaining a desirable economy (or polity, kinship sphere, or culture) has to be interested in simultaneously attaining compatible, equally desirable relations *throughout* society. In the economy, therefore, we must incorporate structures and procedures that safeguard against sexist, racist, or otherwise socially oppressive arrangements.

The only references to these matters in this book were in discussions of the organization of living units and of workplace caucuses of cultural minorities and women in workplaces. Obviously, a lot is missing. In part, in other works we have treated these issues, including how relations in different dimensions interact and, to a point, what would be desirable goals for kinship, political, cultural, ecological, and international dimensions of social life. References can be found in the sidebar on page 6 of this book. But there is much more work to be done.

Many readers will no doubt share our view that there should be role and material equality between men and women and all social/cultural groups, freedom of sexual preference and respect for diversity of sexual and social choices, freedom for any cultural minority to practice its beliefs without fear of penalty, full political participation for all members of society, full dissemination of information and skills essential to making political decisions, respect for the natural environment both as it affects humanity and in its own right, and an equalization of wealth on an international scale. But more detailed descriptions of cultural, kinship, political, ecological, and international institutions still need to be developed.

## Transition to Participatory Economics

How to move toward a participatory economy is a very different question than how does a well-established participatory economy work. Strategies for building a participatory economy are part of overall strategies for social change. As such, the transition to participatory economics includes how to mobilize people's energy for social change, how to raise consciousness and commitment, whether to pursue electoral, grassroots, or confrontational tactics, what interim institutions to establish, what programs to pursue in other dimensions of social life, and how to overcome various obstacles as they arise. Answers obviously vary depending on the country, obstacles encountered, etc. But even after we begin the "long march" toward participatory economics, it is one thing to have a clear idea of what the finished product should look like and quite another to know what to do in the early stages when old values and habits prevail and skills and decision making experience are unequally distributed.

What makes transition from one economic system to another difficult? For one thing the "playing field" continually alters. Opponents continually use new methods to block change. Not even the most thoroughly prepared movement can foresee all the eventualities of struggle. Moreover, efforts to change economic structures do not evolve independently of influences from a society's political, kinship, and cultural spheres. Even the best prepared movement for economic change will fail if it underestimates or misunderstands the impact of political, cultural, and gender forces. It follows, therefore, that economic activists must be flexible and promote the agendas of activists struggling to change other spheres of social life in compatible directions.

We take it as self-evident that there is little reason to address the details of transition until there is at least broad agreement on "transition to what." Still, goals should certainly inform strategy so, to close, we point out a few general implications of participatory vision for participatory strategy. We begin with four conclusions:

1. Markets, central planning, hierarchical production, and hierarchical consumption all propel coordinator rather than participatory aims.

2. Participatory production requires balanced work complexes and must allow producers to understand the effects their choices have on others as well as themselves.

3. Participatory consumption must reflect sociality while preserving privacy; it must allow consumers to understand the implications of their choices for producers.

4. Participatory allocation must promote collective self-management and solidarity by providing both quantitative and qualitative information about the consequences of economic choices.

But how do these conclusions bear on strategy or transitional program?

## Strategic Principles

Contemporary economic struggle features three major classes pursuing three opposed aims: (1) capitalists trying to maintain capitalism; (2) coordinators trying to establish or maintain coordinator relations; and (3) workers struggling to introduce participatory economics.

Of course, not all members of any class will actively participate, nor will all those who do participate always support movements

Let us lay claim to our birthright liberty, love, *and* delight.
Sheila Rowbotham
*Reclaim the Moon*

Alice: ...would you tell me please which way we should go from here?
The Cat: That depends a good deal on where you want to get to.
—Lewis Carroll
*Alice in Wonderland*

Three passions, simple but overwhelmingly strong, have governed my life: the longing for love, the search for knowledge, and unbearable pity for the suffering of mankind.

—Bertrand Russell
*Autobiography*

representing their class interests. Defections are important, whether workers ignoring their better interests and serving as police for capitalists, or coordinators overcoming their elitism and putting their skills at the service of workers. Nonetheless, these three opposed goals will dominate economic struggle and alternatives.

But while long-term programs deriving from each class vision are contradictory, short-term goals will sometimes coincide. Likewise, each movement will compete for the allegiance of many of the same actors, though on different bases. It follows that an important component of participatory economic strategy will be developing ways to utilize the energies and skills of coordinators while never compromising the working-class character, culture, and content of the movement for participatory economics.

### Formation Of Councils

A participatory economic strategy must emphasize forming and strengthening councils of workers and consumers. If economic change is to emphasize collective self-management, these institutions must become primary vehicles of the struggle for participatory aims. This would begin with grassroots community movements that organize neighborhood consumer councils which collaborate with neighborhood political, gender, and cultural struggles. Progressive organizers in workplaces should organize workers' councils with autonomous women's and minority caucuses. Obviously, these early councils would only address some issues, depending on the circumstances organizers face. But struggles in the workplace must win reforms that give workers ever greater say over their worklife and increasing confidence, security, and institutional strength for pursuing further participatory gains.

### Pursuit Of Collective Self-management

The struggle for change must always enhance workers' decision-making authority and increase workers' access to, understanding of, and utilization of information about their workplaces and the economy as a whole. Economic struggles in which workers participate as shock troops while "experts" monopolize decision making may win some short-run victories, but they will strengthen coordinator tendencies and not prepare workers to manage their own lives.

Likewise, consumer struggles must seek not only to improve consumers' well being, but to develop their strength. Networks of consumer councils must campaign against ecological destruction and other inefficient and antisocial aspects of market systems as well as fighting against higher prices and unsafe products.

### Pursuit Of Solidarity

Programs must steer producers to look beyond their own circumstances to the well-being of other producers and consumers as well. Programs that win gains for workers in one unit at the expense of other workers or consumers will not create the psychological or social conditions required to win participatory aims.

Thus, participatory workplace programs might emphasize price controls as well as wage increases, product improvements as well as workplace health and safety, and corporate responsibility for neighborhood and regional well-being as well as job benefits that enhance the quality of work life.

Similarly, consumer struggles should include demands not to cut wages as well as for price controls. Likewise, demands for better products should be coupled to demands for improved working conditions for producers.

### Definition Of Job Structures

Workplace organizing must emphasize the desirability of equitable job complexes even while capitalist owners and coordinators obstruct their formation.

As councils form they can begin to demand training in multiple skills and changes in technology to promote teamwork rather than fragmentation. It is also important that movement organizations and institutions incorporate participatory norms in defining their own work complexes and decision-making processes. Institutions that we control must serve as practical examples of the advantages of equitable, participatory arrangements. Deviation from participatory norms where we can do better is both hypocritical and demoralizing. It will not accomplish much to proclaim the virtues of equity and participation while establishing "progressive" institutions that embody hierarchical divisions of labor.

### Control Of Information

A movement for participatory economics must democratize the use of computers and computer-recorded information. A consumer and producer movement that understands how computers can help their members keep abreast of information and affect decisions will be better able to pursue its goals than a movement that abandons these tools to technocrats.

To ignore computer and information technology, or to assume that these technologies will automatically become democratized, will only ensure that they are dominated by coordinators, thereby diminishing the chances of attaining participatory aims. We envision consumer and producer councils beginning with computer networking and ultimately building facilities for participatory planning.

### Allocation

Participatory movements must continually highlight the problems generated by markets and central planning. The blame for ecological destruction must be laid at the feet of market allocation and technocratic instrumentalism. The bankruptcy of central plan-

ning must be seen as the consequence of its obstruction of popular participation rather than an improper balancing of centralization and decentralization in a new technological era.

Struggles to use participatory structures alongside markets and hierarchical planning can help demonstrate why participatory allocation will solve problems that markets and central planning create.

### Alignment With Other Movements

Economic and other activists must evolve interactive strategies. This will have profound implications for the ways economic struggles treat issues of gender, race, ecology, and international relations, not only at the level of demands and appeals to constituencies, but at the level of organizational forms and movement culture. One principle that should be applied in all movement work is respect for the legitimacy and strategic priority of liberatory struggles in all areas of life. There must be no presumption on the part of participatory economic activists that their struggle is more important than efforts to transform gender, political, race, ecological, or international relations. The success of participatory economic movements rests on the successes of liberatory movements organizing to transform other spheres of social life just as much as the success of those movements depends on a participatory transformation of the economy. Presumptions about the theoretical and strategic priority of class over politics, race, and gender in progressive social change is unwarranted and has long proved counter-productive to establishing movement relations needed for eliminating political, gender, race, *and* class oppressions.

These implications undermine fundamental beliefs of Marxist and Leninist strategic approaches, as we discussed in the Prologue. Therefore, we believe the vision elaborated in this book has profound implications for the strategic approaches movements should employ to attain new goals. Of course it will be activists in all phases of economic struggle who will refine the participatory vision, as well as elaborate strategies for attaining it.

### Transition from Coordinator to Participatory Economics

We have argued that markets and central planning impede participatory economic values, and that societies that do not have councils, balanced job complexes, payment according to effort, and popular participation in allocation do not elevate workers and consumers to power over their own lives. In other books (see page 6) we have considered these matters, as well as other issues of strategy, in greater depth, addressing relations between workers and coordinators, and among factions of coordinators in the Soviet Union, China, and Cuba. We explained that often struggle continues over the "coordinator versus the workers' road" long after capitalism is overthrown. Two questions arise:

1. What might a transition from a coordinator to a participatory economy look like?

2. How could workers advance the cause of participatory economics in post-capitalist settings where coordinator rule is not fully entrenched?

The experience of Solidarity *in its early years* in Poland provides information regarding the first question. Solidarity's early efforts included building a network of councils based primarily in production yet sensitive to consumers needs. Further, Solidarity's early demands, and the tone and language of the movement, emphasized not only material changes affecting income distribution and investment policies, but also qualitative changes in social relations regarding justice and participation.

Indeed, the experience of Solidarity in the early 1980s, and of movements in Hungary in the 1950s and Czechoslovakia in the 1960s, as well as their subsequent failures, suggest that many of the strategic guidelines and pitfalls outlined above for transition from capitalism to participatory economics apply also to the transition from coordinator to participatory economics. On the one hand, this shows how incomplete the guidelines are, since coordinator and capitalist economies are quite different and detailed programs for transforming these two types of economies must differ in important respects. But the overlap also shows that struggles for full economic liberation waged in the two kinds of economy are similar in important respects as well.

In a coordinator economy, as in a capitalist one, participatory strategy must emphasize:

1. Formation of producer and consumer councils.

2. Reforms that improve the terrain from which new struggles are waged, that empower working people, and that demystify expertise.

3. Increasing solidarity among workers, consumers, and liberatory movements in all spheres of social life.

4. Definition of equitable job complexes.

5. Democratic dissemination of information and skills.

6. Criticism of markets and central planning and espousal of participatory planning as a superior alternative.

Whether we are talking about transforming a capitalist economy or a coordinator economy, regrettably we are talking about an economic revolution that will likely involve intense class struggle. However differently they will defend themselves, capitalists and coordinators are both likely to steadfastly cling to power and

> An hour's listening disclosed the fanatical intolerance of minds sealed against new ideas, new facts, new feelings, new attitudes, new hints at ways to live. They denounced books they had never read, people they had never known, ideas they could never understand, and doctrines whose names they could not pronounce. Communism, instead of making them leap forward with fire in their hearts to become masters of ideas and life, had frozen them at an even lower level of ignorance than had been theirs before they met Communism.
> —Richard Wright

> To present the Russian regime as "socialist" or as a "worker's state" as do both the left and the right in an almost universal complicity, or even to discuss its nature in reference to socialism to determine at what points and to what degree it deviates from it, represents one of the most horrendous enterprises of mystification known in history.
> —Cornelius Castoriadis

In our hands is placed a power greater
than their hoarded gold
Greater than their mighty armies
magnified a thousandfold;
We can bring to birth a new world
from the ashes of the old,
For the Union makes us strong.
—*Solidarity Forever*

privilege. As the "Revolutions of 1989" have demonstrated, transitions *between* coordinator and capitalist economies, in either direction, can occur without excessive disruption if large segments of ruling elites in either system fall on hard times and become convinced that change is in their interests as well. But transitions from *either* coordinator or capitalist economies *to* a participatory economy will inevitably be much more confrontational. While an oversimplification, the reason is obvious. Changing elites—especially when many individuals can successfully change one elite hat for another—is a different affair from eliminating privileged elites altogether. In any case, minimizing the human cost of liberation will be a high priority of strategic planning.

In a situation such as Cuba's, where coordinator and working-class tendencies continue to vie with one another with no final resolution between them, there may be moves to reduce income differentials without any effort to define equitable job complexes. Different factions may struggle over what types of incentives to use and the role of planners. The national government may employ authoritarian central forms alongside more democratic local forms. Struggles against chauvinist consciousness may be waged even while patriarchal divisions of labor are being recreated in the economy. Experiments in cultural diversity might coexist with efforts to impose artistic or literary uniformity. Transition could conceivably occur without too great disruption, as compared to the situation for established coordinator and capitalist economies, if working class forces gained strength in the state and economy simultaneously.

But whatever other factors might influence the balance of forces between those favoring liberating outcomes and those favoring new hierarchies, in any such situation, in *all* existing economies, one disadvantage progressives face is that, to date, the only well-established models for revolutionary social transformation have emphasized nonliberating forms. When the dust of battle settles and the time for construction arrives, the only textbooks and blueprints available deny the possibility of egalitarian and participatory outcomes. Struggle always seems to pit pragmatists with answers against activists with hopes. One side presents blueprints for how to organize the economy and its units; the other side complains that the blueprints fall short of liberatory expectations. We hope our attempt to flesh out the participatory vision will give substance to libertarian hopes.

# Glossary

ACCOUNTING MONEY: Each individual has a "dollar" income recorded in the economy's computer system. The income will be above or below average if the actor is borrowing or lending, or works more or less than average. When an individual or unit proposes receipt of some good, it spends "accounting money" to get it. Every unit and individual can spend up to its income each year, each expenditure being deducted from its account. No cash changes hands, the computer record of remaining income merely decreases with each new expenditure. Likewise, accounting money does not earn interest.

ALLOCATION: The process determining how much of each good is produced and how it is distributed among different users. Markets, central planning, and participatory planning are different systems of allocation.

BALANCED JOB COMPLEX: A collection of tasks within a workplace that is comparable in its burdens and benefits and in its impact on the worker's ability to participate in decision making to all other job complexes in that workplace. Workers have responsibility for a job complex in their main workplace, and often for additional tasks outside to balance their overall work responsibilities with those of other workers in society.

BORROW: An individual can consume more than his or her workload warrants on condition of consuming less or working more in the future to pay off the loan.

CAPITALIST CLASS: Those who own the means of production in capitalist economies.

CCFB—COLLECTIVE CONSUMPTION FACILITATION BOARD: A group of workers organized to provide information and, when requested, advice and guidance to consumption units re collective consumption options.

CENTRAL PLANNING: An allocation system wherein a group we call coordinators develops a plan for work units to carry out. While they may take citizens' preferences into account, the coordinators make the final decisions themselves.

CFB—CONSUMPTION FACILITATION BOARD: A group of workers organized to provide information and advice to consumers re their personal options.

COLLECTIVE CONSUMPTION: Consumption undertaken by groups of individuals acting together and sharing responsibility for the cost (in accounting money), such as playground equipment for a neighborhood park or a new theatre complex for a city.

COORDINATOR CLASS: Planners, administrators, technocrats, and other conceptual workers who monopolize the information and decision-making authority necessary to determine economic outcomes. An intermediate class in capitalism; the ruling class in coordinator economies such as the Soviet Union, China, and Yugoslavia.

COORDINATOR ECONOMY: An economy in which a class of experts/technocrats/managers/conceptual workers monopolizes decision-making authority while traditional workers carry out their orders.

EFB—EMPLOYMENT FACILITATION BOARD: A group of workers who assist people wishing to change their place of work.

HFB—HOUSING FACILITATION BOARD: A group of workers who assist people wishing to change their residence.

IFB—ITERATION FACILITATION BOARD: A group of workers who provide information to participants in participatory planning—indicative prices, levels of supply and demand, qualitative information, etc.—for each iteration (or round) of the planning process.

INCOME: The amount of "accounting money" allotted to a person each year. Income for any individuals or unit would be average or more or less depending on loans, debts, special need, and work load.

INDICATIVE PRICES: Prices indicating the social costs and benefits associated with the use of goods or services. Initial indicative prices would be set at the outset of planning by IFBs based on the prior year's final prices and expected changes. Indicative prices would change from round to round in the planning process in response to excess demands and supplies becoming increasingly more accurate estimates of true social costs and benefits.

ITERATIVE PLANNING: A planning process that more or less repeats the same decision-making and calculating procedures a number of times, each time drawing closer to a final plan. Each new round of the process is a new iteration.

JOB COMPLEX: The collection of tasks comprising an individual's work assignment. All economies have job complexes, which may be unbalanced regarding desirability and empowerment, as in capitalism and coordinatorism, or balanced as in participatory economics.

PARTICIPATORY PLANNING: A social, iterative planning process in which producers and consumers propose and revise their own economic activities in such a way as to yield an equitable and efficient plan.

PARTICIPATORY PRICES: The prices generated by a participatory planning process. The same as indicative prices.

PFB—PRODUCTION FACILITATION BOARD: A group of workers who provide information and guidance to production units about technological options.

QUALITATIVE INFORMATION: A list of the human effects of work and or consumption, people's feelings about it, their reasons for unusual requests, etc.

SLACK: Extra resources, goods, and labor set aside in the plan to take care of possible contingencies.

SOCIAL BENEFITS TO SOCIAL COST RATIO: The social value of the outputs a workplace proposes to provide divided by the social cost of the inputs they propose to use. The ratio allows firms to see how their efforts and efficiency rank alongside national averages.

UFB—UPDATING FACILITATION BOARD: A group of workers who identify and propose changes in a plan after it is agreed on but which become necessary during the plan's implementation.

## About South End Press

South End Press is a nonprofit, collectively run book publisher with over 150 titles in print. Since our founding in 1977, we have tried to meet the needs of readers who are exploring, or are already committed to, the politics of fundamental social change.

Our goal is to publish books that encourage critical thinking and constructive action on the key political, cultural, social, economic, and ecological issues shaping life in the United States and the world. In this way, we hope to give expression to a wide diversity of democratic social movements and to provide an alternative to the products of corporate publishing.

If you would like a free catalog of South End Press books or information about our membership program—which offers two free books and a 40% discount on all titles—please write us at South End Press, 116 Saint Botolph Street, Boston, MA 02115.

### Other Books of Interest Available From South End Press

*Liberating Theory*, by Michael Albert, Leslie Cagan, Noam Chomsky, Robin Hahnel, Mel King, Lydia Sargent, and Holly Sklar—a collectively authored presentation of a perspective for understanding gender, race, politics, and class relations regarding history, vision, and strategy.

*Marxism and Socialist Theory*, by Michael Albert and Robin Hahnel—a critique of Marxist theory and vision including discussion of alternatives for the U.S.

*Socialism Today and Tomorrow*, by Michael Albert and Robin Hahnel—a critique of Soviet, Chinese, and Cuban practice and a presentation of alternative vision regarding economics, culture, kinship, and politics.

*Socialist Visions*, edited by Stephen Shalom—essays and rejoinders on a future vision for U.S. institutions.

*From the Ground Up: Essays on Grassroots and Workplace Democracy*, by C. George Benello—applying values of self-management and participation in social and economic contexts.

*Behind the Silicon Curtain: The Seductions of Work in a Lonely Era*, by Dennis Hayes—the production of information-age tools and its social implications.

*Race, Gender and Work: A Multicultural History of Women in the United States*, by Teresa Amott and Julie Matthaei—the many dimensioned experience of women in the workplace.

*Remaking Society: Pathways to a Green Future*, by Murray Bookchin—incorporating an ecological sensibility in economic and social institutions.